A Prince
among Dogs

A Prince
among Dogs

and Other Stories *of* the Dogs We Love

Callie Smith Grant

Revell
Grand Rapids, Michigan

Published by Fleming H. Revell
a division of Baker Publishing Group
P.O. Box 6287, Grand Rapids, MI 49516-6287

Printed in the United States of America

Library of Congress Cataloging-in-Publication Data
A prince among dogs : and other stories of the dogs we love / [compiled by] Callie Smith Grant.
  p. cm.
Includes bibliographical references.
ISBN 10: 0-8007-5867-6 (pbk.)
ISBN 978-0-8007-5867-7 (pbk.)
  1. Dog owners. 2. Dogs—Religious aspects—Christianity. 3. Pets—Religious aspects—Christianity. 4. Animals—Religious aspects—Christianity. I. Grant, Callie Smith.
BV4596.A54P75 2007
248.2′9—dc22   2007027297

To my editor, Vicki Crumpton,
good and patient friend
to animals and writers

 **Contents**

Foreword

H. Norman Wright

A dog: companion, friend, protector, playmate, and life-changer. Dogs add a dimension to our lives that otherwise would be just a vacant spot. They work for us, guard us, play with us, entertain us, love us, keep us company, and change our lives. That's one of the reasons we like to read about them.

I was delighted to be asked to read this manuscript, and then I discovered I couldn't put it down . . . and neither will you. My resolve to read one chapter at a time crumbled as I became engaged by these stories. It's a book about dogs, but it's more than that. It's a slice of life as it really is—families, difficult times, sadness, joy, losses, and additions. You'll laugh because you've experienced the delights of a dog. You'll say, "I've been there," "My dog did that," "I remember when . . ." and "I hadn't thought about that for years."

This is a book to activate memories, childhood events, family interactions, and just how much a dog can fulfill your life. You may find tears making their appearance with some of the good-byes you read. But you wouldn't miss the experience for anything.

Get ready for an enjoyable journey that may encourage you to reach out and pet your dog, and if you don't have one, to consider opening your heart and home to one.

Introduction

Callie Smith Grant

A friend of mine collected first-edition Jack London books. He was stunned that I'd become an adult without ever having read London's *The Call of the Wild*. "You like dogs," he said. "Read this," and he handed me one of his first editions. Flattered that he'd trust me with such a prize, I sat in the sun the next day and read it straight through. These many years later, one scene still remains with me; it's in the chapter "For the Love of a Man."

The story takes place in the gold rush days of the Far North. The hero, a man named Thornton, has a marvelous sled dog named Buck. One day in a gold camp full of prospectors, some macho bragging commences around the subject of the sled dogs. One thing leads to another, and Thornton finds himself reluctantly agreeing to wager a thousand dollars' worth of gold dust that Buck can pull a thousand pounds of gear on a sled for the distance of one hundred yards.

Thornton is conflicted, of course. Buck is strong, but Thornton isn't sure if Buck is *that* strong. More important, Thornton deeply loves the dog and doesn't want the dog to hurt himself. So Thornton doesn't want to go through with the bet. But he is surrounded by gold rush men, and—macho moments being what they are—he doesn't back down.

In all the excitement before the actual pull, Thornton kneels down in front of his dog Buck:

> He took his head in his two hands and rested cheek to cheek. . . . He whispered in his ear. "As you love me, Buck. As you love me," was what he whispered. Buck whined with suppressed eagerness.[1]

I have always remembered that intimate moment between human and dog—the "As you love me," followed by Buck's response of anticipation. While gambling on an animal's strength would be repugnant to most of us, this scene nevertheless has always shown me the beautiful, mysterious connection between people and dogs, a kind of connection we have with no other creature.

And that wager? Of course Buck comes through and pulls that weight the full distance. Amid all the chaos of the victory, Thornton falls to his knees in front of his dog and openly weeps. Then comes another intimate moment, a both playful and meaningful moment, the kind of moment that helped bring the wolf to man thousands of years ago:

Buck seized Thornton's hand in his teeth. Thornton shook him back and forth. As though animated by a common impulse, the onlookers drew back to a respectful stance; nor were they again indiscreet enough to interrupt.[2]

If you have ever loved a dog and been loved back, you understand.

We've had this love affair with our dogs for thousands of years. During these years, many times our Creator has sent the right dog to the right place at the right time. This book is full of such stories—stories of relationships between humans and their best friend, the dog.

Finding and reading these stories was a pleasure. They made me remember all the dogs in my life. They made me want to adopt lots of dogs. Sometimes they made me laugh, often they made me cry, and since I tend to read in coffeehouses, it got a little embarrassing. These stories made me appreciate that fifth day of creation in a whole new light. Truly, what a creative day that was to produce this noble animal.

My hope is that these stories make you as happy as they've made me—and at least a fraction as happy as our dogs make us.

A Prince among Dogs

Melody Carlson

No one ever knew it to look at him, but somehow this scraggly little black mutt managed to live up to his name: Prince.

Now, let it be known that we did not name him Prince. If he'd been our dog right from the start, we probably would have named him something much more appropriate, like Scruffy or Scrappy or Scamp. But no, he came to us with the name and "only for a short visit."

His owner, Julie, was an exchange student from Singapore, and she'd found the poor puppy literally lying in the street gutter. She told us how he'd been wet and cold and hungry, and despite her apartment's no pets rule, she had rescued him and taken him in. But after several weeks of hiding the forbidden dog, she brought him to our house "for a short visit."

> Ever consider what our dogs must think of us? I mean, here we come back from a grocery store with the most amazing haul—chicken, pork, half a cow. They must think we're the greatest hunters on earth!
>
> *Anne Tyler*

"Just for a couple of weeks," she promised me, "until I can figure something else out."

But after we'd spent a couple of weeks doggy-sitting, our friend Julie pleaded with us to keep her doggy for good. "You have a yard and a fence," she pointed out. "And I'll come to visit every week."

Of course, she didn't have to push too hard since our boys (ages four and five at the time) had already fallen in love with this peppy little puppy. In fact, we were all taken by the sweet little mutt (a mix of Scotty and other terrier and who knew what else), but we weren't too crazy about the name. "Prince" sounded so formal—more like the name of a German shepherd, Great Dane, or Doberman pinscher. Not a scraggly little black mutt.

Just the same, our family adopted the dog "formerly known as Prince," and although we all tried to come up with a name more fitting, we seemed to be stuck with Prince.

Before too long Prince revealed some of his princely character to our family. It started when our younger son Luke was sick in bed with the flu. Now, Prince didn't usually go upstairs where the boys' rooms were. He usually stuck to me like glue since I was the one who fed him. But on this particular day he disappeared. When I went upstairs to take Luke some juice and check his fever, there was Prince, resting quietly beside my sick boy.

At first I thought maybe Prince was ill too (could dogs get the flu?). But his tail wagged happily when he saw me, and he seemed perfectly fine. He didn't leave Luke's side until Luke began feeling better. That's when I began wondering if we should start calling our dog "Dr. Prince."

Now, if this had happened only once, we might have chalked it up to a fluke or coincidence, but the same thing happened again and again. Whenever anyone in our family was sick, Prince would be right by that person's side, almost as if it was his job to take care of them until they recovered. It was incredible to see this normally active dog put aside his romping needs to display this kind of amazing canine compassion for an ailing family member.

But perhaps the most remarkable Prince memory I have is of the time one of our cats (which Prince normally had little use for) had been hit by a car. Pepper's injured leg was bandaged, and we put him in a cardboard box with a blanket, hoping he would rest and heal with time. And sure enough, when I went to check on Pepper's condition, there was Prince, right there in the box with him. He was peacefully curled up right next to Pepper, keeping the cat warm. It was the strangest thing to see. Even our other cat hadn't gone to that much trouble for his feline friend.

Our little Prince lived for nearly sixteen years. And he was loyal and true to our family the entire time. Even in his final days, when he was in pain and nearly blind, I knew that he would lay down his little life for any of us. By then we had all come to realize that his name hadn't been a mistake at all. Without a doubt, our little mutt had been named appropriately—for he truly was a Prince among dogs.

Schoen

Marilyn Martyn McAuley

Answering the phone, I heard my husband ask, "Honey, how do you feel about my bringing home a dog for us?"

"What kind of dog?" I asked. I liked little dogs like the cockers and "Heinz 57" mutts I had grown up with. But large dogs terrified me. I'd been bitten by a large dog once. I would even cross the street or go a block out of my way to avoid walking by a suspicious dog.

Dan said, "He's beautiful and fully trained."

"Fully trained? What kind of dog is it?" I asked again. I felt wary of how this conversation was going.

"He's a purebred with papers, he has completed obedience training, he is only two years old, and they are giving him to us."

"Dan, why aren't you answering my question?" My apprehension was growing.

He finally said, "He's a German shepherd."

I remembered kids in my middle school who had a German shepherd. He was huge. They used to ride him like a pony. But that dog terrified me. That old memory dredged up all the fear I had felt then.

"Honey, are you there?" Dan asked.

"Yes—well, you know how frightened I am of those dogs. What's his name?"

"Schoen. It's German for beautiful, and he really is. He looks just like the dog in the Rin Tin Tin movies. Well, here's the deal. I have to decide now because the owner won't let him stay in their home any longer. It's the pet of one of my students. She's heartbroken, and I'm the first one she's asked to take him. If we don't, he'll go to the pound."

"Why can't they keep him?"

"Schoen doesn't like the mailman. Today he crashed through the screen door to take off after him. Schoen had been threatening to do this for some time, and today the open front door allowed him to escape. If you don't want me to bring him home, then say so, because I can't keep her waiting."

"Okay, bring him home. The boys have been asking for a dog. But please have him on a leash when you come in the house, okay? I'll need to warm up to him from a distance." My fear of the breed gave in to my compassion for the dog needing a home. I certainly didn't want him to go to the pound!

I told John and David a dog was coming home with Daddy. They were five and six years old and just the right age for having a pet. As they waited on the front steps, they thought Daddy would never get home. Personally, I couldn't believe how little time it took him.

I heard the car pull in. I looked out the kitchen window to see a handsome tricolored dog with huge ears perfectly straight and pointing in alert mode as he jumped out of our station wagon. He truly was beautiful. Schoen had made his first impression on me, and it was favorable. But I also felt my heart beating much too fast and knew he would immediately sense my fear. How could I calm down to meet him and not have him jump me? I breathed a prayer for help. God knew my fear but also my desire to become friends with this dog.

The front door opened and in walked Schoen, on his leash as promised. I stood my ground behind the dining room table. The boys enjoyed petting him. They had not been given a reason to fear dogs. Dan cautioned them to be gentle and let Schoen get to know them. I noticed Schoen enjoyed their attention and didn't try to harm them. That helped me a great deal.

"Sit," Dan ordered. Schoen sat. Oh, he was such a regal dog. I wanted to go to him, but I couldn't stop trembling. Finally I made the move from behind the table. As I approached him, he became excited.

Dan said, "He's just eager to meet you."

Fear still had me by the throat. Dan calmed Schoen down and then calmed me down. I finally managed to pet the dog, and he acted the perfect gentleman. Great relief flooded me.

Dan introduced Schoen to each room in the house, then took him outside to walk the perimeter of our property, front and back, so he would feel at home in his new yard. But the most significant event took place after we were all in bed later that night.

I lay in bed upstairs, listening to Schoen pace the floor by the front door. His nails clicked on the hardwood floor, back and forth. He wouldn't rest. Finally, around midnight, I got up and went downstairs. My heart ached for him. I knew that he missed his family—the only family he had ever known. He stood at the front door looking through the glass panel, longing to be on the other side.

He turned when he heard me. The needs of an animal in distress overpowered my fear of being alone with him. "Schoen," I said softly, "it's going to be okay. We love you and will take good care of you." All the while I petted him and stroked his coat. But his eyes would not leave the window.

It was the beginning of summer, and the evenings were pleasant. I got Schoen's leash and hooked it to his collar. Could I control him if I took him outside? Instinctively, I knew I had to take him out. I opened the door. He was so excited. "Schoen, be good now," I said with quiet authority. He pulled eagerly on the leash, and I held on with all my strength as I quietly closed the screen door. I sat on the top step, put my arm around the dog, and ordered him to sit. He sat, but not without lifting first one paw and then the other.

I kept my arm around him, holding the leash with my other hand. I sat close to him, touching his warm body and feeling the tension within him, knowing

> I wonder if other dogs think poodles are members of a weird religious cult.
>
> *Rita Rudner*

at first opportunity he'd be down the street and headed for home.

"You want to go home, don't you, boy?" He understood me. His nose pointed in the right direction. "So you are very intelligent as well as beautiful, aren't you?" He anxiously moved his head, keeping his focus pointed east. His eyes, his ears, his attention and reactions told me this dog understood far more than I had any idea. It encouraged me to continue talking. His first family had cared for him well, so I knew he had learned a fair-sized vocabulary.

"You know, Schoen, I am afraid too. You're afraid of not being with the people you love, and I'm afraid of being with such a big dog." He looked at me a moment, then returned to his vigil. "It's going to be okay. You will be happy with us. You will love playing with the boys, and I bet you'll grow to love us and even protect us." Suddenly he lay down by me, but he kept his head pointed toward home.

"Oh, that's a good boy, Schoen. We will do fun things together. The boys will play ball with you; we'll go to the beach, and go camping, and take walks in the park." At that he acted like he wanted to say, "Okay, let's go!" He definitely knew that word. He had played in a park across the street from his first home. I continued talking, repeating myself and letting him get familiar with my voice.

After a while we just sat quietly. Finally he rested his head on his paws. I scratched him under his chin and around his ears—the softest fur I've ever felt. "Schoen, I think we're going to be the best of buddies." Both of us overcame our fears that night as we finally relaxed and enjoyed sitting together.

It had been a couple of hours. I stood and Schoen sat up. "I guess we'd better go back in the house and get some sleep, don't you think, Schoen?" Compliantly, he turned with me, and we went in. I released the leash, laid it on the counter, and courageously took his head in my hands, placed my face on his big head, and told him I loved him. He licked my cheek. Our bonding had begun. "Goodnight, Schoen." He watched as I went up the stairs. I crawled into bed and listened. Before long I heard a sound I would soon recognize as contentment—a *ha-rumpf* as he lowered his large frame to the floor to go to sleep. I smiled. It took Schoen only two hours to help me overcome my fear of large dogs.

Taffy, the Unexpected Guard Dog

Anne C. Watkins

But I don't want a dog," I protested. I stared down at the bundle of fuzzy golden hair my brother had shoved into my arms. The puppy, a tiny female, wiggled and squirmed and tried to lick my chin.

"You need her," my brother replied. "It'll do you good to have something to occupy your mind. And you won't have to worry about buying her dog food for a while." He plunked down a huge sack of puppy food on the porch, hopped into his truck, and drove away with a cheerful wave.

I looked down at the little face gazing up at me and sighed. "Well, girl," I said, "looks like we're stuck with each other." The puppy struggled to get down. I set her on the porch, and she immediately began nibbling the toe of my tennis shoe. In spite of myself, I laughed out loud.

As the days passed, the puppy, whom I named Taffy, found her way into my heart. She exuded energy, and everything that wasn't tied down in the house ended up in the front yard. Before long I wondered how I had ever managed without her cheerful presence. And my brother was right. She had given me something to think about besides the miserable mess my life had been for the last year.

I had just spent several months in a domestic violence shelter, and though I was safe there, I felt stifled. I longed for a place of my own. Now I found myself living in a tiny mobile home on my father's property, trying to get my life back in order. It was the hardest thing I'd ever faced, and I wasn't sure I was strong enough to do it. But my family was pulling for me, and all sorts of folks were sending up prayers on my behalf. My nerves still jangled with every unexpected noise, but I clenched my jaw and struggled along. At the same time, Taffy grew into a lovely medium-sized dog and became my constant companion. Her joyful, silly personality anchored me.

Wintertime rolled around, and one night the weather turned extremely cold. Chilly fingers of wind crept through the loose-fitting windows of my bedroom and stirred around my face. Hoping to soak up a little extra heat, I snuggled against Taffy's shaggy body. Underneath the thick comforter I was warm, and on top, where Taffy lay curled, floated a small ring of cozy air. Eyes heavy, I drew her close. She sighed in contentment and rested her head on my chest. We settled in to sleep.

Suddenly Taffy stiffened. Her head snapped up, and I felt the hair on her neck rise. Before I could move, she leaped off the bed. Every hair on her body bristled, and with slow, deliberate steps, she stalked toward the back door that was just a few feet from my bedroom. Wide awake now, I huddled in fear, wondering what lurked outside.

A low growl rumbled from deep inside her as she paced up and down the narrow hallway. Once or twice she froze, her eyes focused on the back door. Every sharp tooth in her mouth gleamed as she drew her lips back in a fierce snarl. I couldn't believe the intensity of her growls. She was no longer the happy-go-lucky little dog I knew so well. This dog was a furious, vicious guard dog, and she meant business.

Choking back a wave of bone-deep terror, I realized that I had nothing in the house to use as a weapon. The only thing I could think of was a big kitchen knife, and it was all the way at the other end of the trailer. Almost nauseated by fear, I wrapped my arms around my pillow and prayed that the door locks would hold if someone tried to force their way through.

Taffy continued to prowl the hall, her stiff-legged, exaggerated walk intimidating to see. The harsh snarls ripping from her sounded as if they came from a much larger, stronger animal. From time to time, she turned to face me. We made eye contact, and the warm, loving

The Politically Correct Nomenclature . . . Sort Of

There's a standing joke about pet owners and their amazing pets: who really "owns" whom? Animal breed magazines indirectly suggest that nobody owns anybody by the fact that they tend to use the word *guardian*. That is to say that when you have a pet in your life, you are not the pet's owner but rather the pet's "guardian." Of course, when that pet is a dog, doesn't it beg the question: who's the "guardian" of whom?

gaze I was used to seeing was now hard and angry. I received the distinct impression that she was telling me to stay put. I did.

After what seemed like a very long time, Taffy relaxed. Her bristled back and neck softened, and she stopped growling. She made a few more passes up and down the hall, sniffed around the back door, then came and hopped up on the bed. She wagged her tail and licked my hand. "Everything okay now, girl?" I whispered. In reply, she flopped over on her side and wriggled up against me, satisfied that the danger had passed. Still shaken, I settled down to try to snatch a few hours of uneasy sleep.

The next morning I bundled up and walked all around the house, searching for clues to what had set Taffy off. Then my blood turned to ice. Just underneath my bedroom window lay a pile of cigarette butts. My knees went weak, and I collapsed against the side of the trailer.

I had no doubt that whoever had been out there had meant to harm me but had been foiled by one small, determined dog. I looked up from the cigarette butts to see Taffy trotting around the yard, enjoying the crisp morning air. She looked innocent and playful, but I had seen what she could become if the person she loved was in danger. Her fluffy golden hair, warm brown eyes, and goofy personality were wrapped around a brave, fearless heart. And I almost lost out on her because I didn't think I wanted a dog.

The Night Buster Was a Dolphin

Lonnie Hull DuPont

I n 1996 my husband Joe and I flew from our home in San Francisco to my parents' home in Florida. My stepdad, who had raised me since childhood, needed a very serious surgery. He was eighty years old and was told that he had a 50–50 chance of pulling through. It was serious enough that Joe and I kept our return ticket open and packed clothes that would be appropriate for a funeral.

Mom picked us up at the airport the night before the operation. Their dog Buster was in the car and simply beside himself with joy at seeing us. "This is good," said Mom, nodding at the dog. "He's been depressed ever since your dad went into the hospital. These days he stays under a table when we're home."

That didn't sound like Buster at all. A mix of schnauzer, poodle, and cocker spaniel, he was a friendly, energetic dog and smart as a whip. He was a comical-looking thing; his back legs seemed considerably longer than his front legs, and his short, stocky body was covered with long black hair and two shocks of white that streaked diagonally across his face and belly. This gave him an off-kilter look, and he wore it well. Bright little black eyes flashed at us from under a lot of eyebrow hair that sort of stuck out from his face. All this housed an even-tempered and outgoing disposition. And he adored Dad.

My folks had heard about this runt of the litter when he was just old enough to leave his momma. On a whim they went to see him. As soon as Buster the pup saw Dad, he ran to him. Dad scooped him up, and the little guy curled right up to Dad's breast. Both Dad and the dog were smitten right away.

Not that Buster only loved Dad. He wanted to be cuddled like a baby by Mom each morning, even though he was actually a little too big to be a lap dog. And he truly liked everyone, as long as they weren't encroaching on his territory. To be honest, I liked going home to visit Buster as much as I liked visiting my folks. But Dad was alpha dog from the beginning for Buster. And Buster went everywhere with Dad.

Buster was only two years old when I brought my new husband home to my family. Buster growled a little at first at this tall male stranger, but I told Joe to sit down, dangle his arm, and let Buster come to him. After enough sniffing to satisfy himself, Buster brought a toy to Joe with a clear invitation to toss it. Joe took the bait and eventually was rolling on the floor with Buster. From then on Buster looked to Joe for a good time.

Our second trip home as a couple was a different time Dad was in the hospital. We spent days with him in his room while Buster waited in the car. Buster would rather sit in a car all day than stay home. My husband, who is not one to sit at all, took on the job of taking Buster out of the car for frequent walks.

One afternoon during that time, Joe was gone an entire hour, so I strolled off to look for him. I found him in the station wagon napping with Buster, the two of them lying spoon fashion, both lightly snoring. This was truly a bonding experience for Buster. After that, even though we only visited my folks once or twice a year, Buster was always thrilled to see Joe. They would play and play, indoors and outdoors. I would venture to say that at those times Joe was honorary alpha dog number two.

Now we were with Mom at a very difficult time, and on the first night, Buster played with Joe almost frantically. But soon the little guy retreated under a table and stayed there most of the time. He did indeed seem depressed.

On the morning of the operation, we left Buster home. We spent a long day waiting at the hospital until finally the surgeon came to us. He reported that Dad had made it through surgery but was not yet out of the woods. He needed to make it through the night first.

Mom and I were allowed to see Dad for a few minutes. I had seen people unconscious and hooked up to machines after surgery before; nobody looks good at such a time. But Dad looked horrible. Mom and I didn't even speak, we were so distressed. When our time was up, we left, gathered up Joe, and drove home in silence.

It was now dark. In the house, we all quietly readied ourselves for bed. Buster raised himself up to greet us, but that was about all. Soon he scooted back under a table and curled away from us.

Restless, Joe offered to run to the store for a few things, and I stayed behind with Mom. I was concerned about her. It was just before Valentine's Day, and Dad had given her flowers and candy that past week in case he didn't make it through the operation. There sat the roses on the table. I was still kind of a newlywed and felt terribly sad for my Mom, who might be losing the love of her life.

We retreated to our bedrooms before Joe returned. I was exhausted, but I could not sleep. All I could think about was how much I did not want to lose my sweet stepdad and, in particular, how much I didn't want my mother to lose her husband. After tossing and turning for a while, I gave up. I quietly left my room and then saw that my mother was also up, sitting in her chair in the living room. Buster was asleep, stretched out under his table.

"I can't sleep," Mom said.

I curled up on the couch. "Neither can I."

She was crying a little. "He looked so awful."

I nodded. "Yes, he did."

We fell quiet. Soon the front door opened, and Joe came in bearing grocery bags. Buster suddenly came to life and jumped all over Joe. Always willing to play, Joe dropped the bags on the table and joined Buster on the floor.

It's hard to explain what happened in the next few minutes. First I must report that a few weeks before, Joe and I had watched a TV documentary in which dolphins were mimicking humans in water. Of course the dolphins only did what they could physically do, but their trainers would make noises or swim a certain way, and the dolphins would mimic them, clearly enjoying themselves. It was fascinating and fun to watch.

Of course Buster is not a dolphin, and I don't recall ever seeing a dog actually mimic a human. But tonight, as Buster looked to Joe for action, Joe rolled on his back and kicked his legs, and Buster flopped down and did the same. My mother and I started laughing.

Now Joe rolled over and lifted his chest up with his legs extended like a seal. Buster did the same. The two of them inched across the carpet this way, bobbing their heads up and down. Mom and I howled.

Joe flopped back on his back and kicked his legs. So did Buster.

This went on for several minutes, back and forth. Mom and I laughed so hard our sides hurt and tears ran down our faces. When finally Joe got tired, Buster allowed himself to be petted, then retreated under the table again.

We three humans continued to giggle and giggle until we finally took ourselves down the hall to our beds. Before I went into Joe's and my room, I hugged my mother and said, "That was a gift, wasn't it?"

She agreed. And we all slept a good night.

So did Dad. Our prayers were answered—he pulled through that night and the next. He was going to make it. But during those days, Buster now refused to eat.

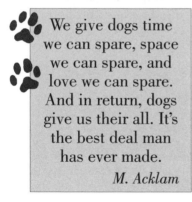

We give dogs time we can spare, space we can spare, and love we can spare. And in return, dogs give us their all. It's the best deal man has ever made.

M. Acklam

On the third day, I stayed home while Mom and Joe went to the hospital. I was reading at the kitchen table when I heard Buster's dog tags. I looked down, and there he sat, looking at me.

"What's up?" I said. "Do you want to go outside?"

No response. He simply looked at me. Well, I thought, I may as well see if he'll eat. I got a piece of leftover steak from the fridge, and he wolfed it down. Heartened, I filled his dish with dog food. He devoured it. I refilled it, and he ate again.

The phone rang as Buster was finishing up. It was Mom.

"Guess what!" she said. "Your Dad just ate for the first time!"

I looked at the dog. "So did Buster."

For the next few days, Buster continued to eat and was a little more himself, though he stayed low-key until Dad came home from the hospital. From then on, Buster took it upon himself never to leave Dad's side. And I truly believe that when Dad passed away four years later, Buster grieved as much as any of us. A few years later my mom passed on, and only two months later, so did Buster.

My parents needed Buster in many ways, and he was an excellent companion for them both, especially as they aged. As for me, I best remember when Buster put on a show for us during a hard time—a mimicking that he never did before or again—that helped his humans laugh and relax and rest up for a better day.

FIVE FAVE DOG BOOKS

Obviously many, many good dog books have been written. But I live in a small space, and these two novels and three works of nonfiction have earned the right to stay on my bookshelves. Presented alphabetically by title:

Animals in Translation by Temple Grandon: The author is a famous animal expert who is also autistic, and her book's purpose is to explain and compare the similarities between how animals process information and how autistic humans process information. So while it's technically not a dog book, it has a great deal in it about dogs, especially in offhand comments about breeds. Fascinating reading told in a direct, matter-of-fact voice.

The Call of the Wild by Jack London: This famous American novelist writes eloquently about dogs in many books and short stories. This one, written from the points of view of both man and dog, has some stunning prose. A strong and handsome sled dog fulfills his purpose with the human in his life, then finds himself drawn to the company of wolves.

The Hidden Life of Dogs by Elizabeth Marshall Thomas: The author is an anthropologist who loves animals. Get past the fact that her own dogs wander all over the place; instead, get into her amazing, well-expressed observations about dogs and what motivates them. This book spent lots of time on the *New York Times* bestseller list. (Cat lovers should get this author's *The Tribe of Tiger* for an equally pleasurable reading experience.)

Lassie Come Home by Eric Knight: The original, break-your-heart story told in such a beautiful way you can almost hear the Scottish burr. This is the book that started it all on television when baby boomers were kids, which in turn kicked in the collie craze of many of our childhoods.

Marley and Me by John Grogan: The subtitle states the true appeal of this *New York Times* bestseller list megahit: *Life and Love with the World's Worst Dog.* We all know dogs love their imperfect humans unconditionally, but what happens when you have to love your dog the same way? Bad-dog Marley reminds us that we truly live in a fallen world. The chapter where Marley flunks dog training class made me—and everyone I know who read it—laugh out loud.

Showing Up at L/J Stables

Chad Allen

It seems like every boarding stable has its own
canine ranch hand. At L/J Stables in Plain City,
Utah, the mantle fell to a splotchy gray and black
mutt named Mac. L/J Stables is where my dad kept
his horses for a few years when I was a kid.

Mac was tall enough to hold a person's hand in his
mouth—something he did regularly—and his face was
shaped like a golden retriever's. I remember seeing
him outflank and out-jump horses in the pasture, but
for all his swiftness and muscular power, he was a
compassionate sort. When he looked at you, he tilted
his head and lowered his eyebrows like a concerned
mother.

Precious few are the friends who show the same
loyalty Mac showed. Not once did he fail to run and
bark out his greeting when I rode my bike down the

road that led to the stable yard. I'd say hi to him as he wagged his tail, and he'd amble beside me.

He was handy with horses too. Sometimes horses will lie down in their stalls in such a way that they can't get their legs underneath them to stand up. More than once Mac heard a horse in distress and ran to the nearest human. Gingerly holding the person's hand in his mouth, Mac would bring help to some poor mare who'd gotten herself into trouble.

On hot days Mac and I would lay down in the shade of a large trampoline in front of the stable keepers' ranch house. Mac let me use his body for a pillow, and I'd stare up through the netting of the trampoline and teach him what shapes the clouds were. "Now, Mac, that one there is a dragon," I'd say. "And that one over there, that's a huge ugly monster." Every now and again Mac would lift up his head and look at me; then he'd drop it to the ground and sigh. I guess he didn't think much of my tutoring.

Looking back, I believe Mac taught me more than I taught him. One thing he taught me was the importance of showing up. Whether he was meeting me on a country road, saving a horse, or giving me his company under the trampoline, Mac always showed up.

I can't help but wonder how things would be different if the rest of the world showed up more often. What if nations always showed up for peace summits? What if CEOs always showed up for work? What if fathers always showed up for dinner?

Mac showed up for another event, and that was to say good-bye. One day Dad got a new job, and we had to move. On my last day at L/J Stables, I told Mac to keep taking care of the horses and helping out with the place. I hugged him and told him I'd miss him and I'd never forget him.

When it was time to go, I walked with him to my bike and gave him a good scratch on the head, and he ran beside me for a while as I rode away for the last time. I looked back, and there he was, looking after me as one friend to another.

I suppose Mac is still showing up for his daily duties, if not at L/J Stables, then somewhere else. It was his nature, and I hope it is mine as well.

My Dog Kramer

Deb Kalmbach

K ramer. My heart warms just thinking about
this fuzzy white bundle of boundless canine
energy. This little dog has taught me volumes
about the unconditional love I desire to emulate. I
can't help but wonder if Kramer was sent to us for
this purpose.

My husband Randy and I own a small video store
in our rural community of Winthrop, Washington.
After watching *My Dog Skip*, a poignant account of a
boy and his beloved dog, I found myself longing for
a dog like Skip. Sure, it would help if he looked like
his movie counterpart, a Jack Russell terrier, but all
I really wanted was the incredible love and devotion
this sweet creature had for his master.

"I want a dog like Skip," I confided to Randy. "He's
the kind of dog I wanted when I was a kid." With five
children, my parents, who had their hands under-

standably full, were quite firm: no pets. I have always felt slightly deprived.

I never dreamed Randy would pick up the phone to call the only breeder listed in the phone book.

"We have one male puppy, a Jack Russell terrier," she said.

Randy told her we'd like to come see him but only to take a look. Becoming parents to a puppy was a major decision. We searched the Web for information about Jack Russells. The official website was less than encouraging. *These are high-strung, willful dogs with compulsive behavior*, said the experts. *They have a mind of their own. At times you'll laugh when you realize they've outwitted you one more time to get their way.*

"I'm not so sure," I lamented. "Those dogs don't sound like Skip. Maybe Hollywood tweaked the story to make him more lovable."

Reluctantly, and against our better judgment, we decided to go anyway—but *only* to see the pup.

Junior, as he had been affectionately named, bounded right up to us as if he knew he was going home. How could we resist those brown eyes, his tail wagging a mile a minute, and the best part of all—he looked just like Skip!

We hadn't intended to take him home, but the breeder persuaded us. "If you want him, you'd better take him now. He needs to bond with you."

Suddenly we were parents of a three-month-old puppy. He lay curled on my lap on the two-hour drive back home. We stopped at Wal-Mart for the unplanned-for supplies: food, dishes, and toys, including the monkey squeak toy another shopper heartily recommended.

So our lives were turned upside down and our hearts inside out with love for Kramer, as we christened him. Of course he had to have a Hollywood name to work in a video store. Every day Randy packed Kramer and his puppy paraphernalia and took him to our store, much to the delight of our customers. "Is Kramer in today?" they'd ask expectantly.

We were amazed at our pet's ability to weave himself into the fabric of our lives, becoming part of everything we did. The routines and rituals of chasing the favorite ball over and over again, growling at the old plastic flowerpot, and riding everywhere in the car with us became part of Kramer's daily schedule.

When the weather turned cold, we ordered a red winter jacket from the Jack Russell terrier catalog. Kramer dutifully put his paws through the black knitted legs and looked like a toddler walking stiff-legged in his snowsuit. That didn't stop him from romping in the snow. He skimmed his nose through the fresh powder, making the most unique set of tracks.

Kramer defied the website's description. Although he exhibited some terrier characteristics—being a tenacious hunter of chipmunks or racing turbo-speed through the house—his nature was sweet and lapdog mellow.

Work like a Dog—or Rather, Work **with** a Dog

Every year Pet Sitters International sponsors "Take Your Dog to Work Day," often abbreviated TYDTWD. It's celebrated on the last Friday in June in the United States. (It's also celebrated in Canada, Australia, New Zealand, and the United Kingdom, but not necessarily on the same day as in the United States.)

Anyone who loves his or her dog would most likely love to take Fido to work. The objective of TYDTWD, however, is not simply to make dog lovers content by having their companion nearby from 9:00 to 5:00. This day's greater objective is to make pet adoptions more common by boosting exposure to animal shelters and breed rescue groups.

Want your workplace to participate? Search the Internet using the phrase "Take Your Dog to Work." You'll find everything from tips for getting corporations involved to guidelines for having Fido hang with you at work. Don't forget the water dish!

Our customers complimented us on our great marketing idea and the making of a town icon. The thought had never occurred to us. A local artist bumped into me at the grocery store one day and said, "I've been thinking about the MGM lion and that I could draw something similar with Kramer." Since then the MGM "Kramer" has graced T-shirts, newspaper ads, and our website.

When Kramer turned one year old, we celebrated with a birthday party at the store. Kramer secretly told me he wanted a chocolate cake with cream cheese frosting, which was a big hit with his guests. They brought dog biscuit gifts and even called on the phone to wish him a happy day.

We chuckle about Kramer's local notoriety. We were hiking one summer afternoon when a complete stranger stopped and asked, "Is this Kramer?" Our dog has even enjoyed stardom in the annual '49ers Days parade, a favorite event in our Western-themed town. We drove the parade route in Randy's old '89 Lincoln Town Car festooned with Kramer banners and balloons. Children lining the one street through town squealed, "Look, there's Kramer!" Randy and I tried not to let it get us down that no one noticed us.

I'm wise enough to perceive that Kramer is more than a marketing gimmick. I think he may be a furry angel sent simply to love us and to help heal our hearts' ragged edges. Perhaps the good Lord sent him to faithfully wait at the end of our long workdays, eyes bright with pure, accepting love. All I know is that our lives are much richer for knowing this sweet friend.

Cindy, a Dog
Who Listened

Kathryn Lay

C indy was my best friend. My mom called her a nuisance, but to me, she was a dog with a personality. At age eleven I fell in love with the tiny, curly-haired dog.

Cindy was smart too. I taught her tricks. She would sit by my feet, and when I put a stick or piece of carrot by her mouth and said, "Chew," she would stand and obey. She loved going for walks with me and my friends. She danced around us as if listening to our conversations about school and clothes and movies we'd seen.

Sometimes I sat with her in the front yard, letting her explore the soft grass. I'd tell her about my friends, the boys I liked, the test I was about to take in history. Cindy would sit and stare at me as if listening to everything I told her.

Then my uncle, my mother's younger brother, came to live with us for a while. He and his wife slept in my room, and I slept on the couch. My mom didn't want Cindy's curly fur all over the living room furniture, so Cindy slept in the utility room in her plush bed. Instead of being beside my bed as usual, she was out of my aunt and uncle's way. I resented their presence and kept Cindy outside with me as much as possible.

> A dog teaches a boy fidelity, perseverance, and to turn around three times before lying down.
>
> *Robert Benchley*

But one afternoon when I went to get her from the back-yard, she wasn't there. The back gate was partly open. Had Cindy been searching for me?

I looked everywhere around the neighborhood, knocking on doors and asking everyone I knew and didn't know if they'd seen her. I called her name, called my friend who always came to me. This time she didn't come.

"Sorry," my uncle said. "I guess when I went through the gate to check something on my car, I forgot to close it completely."

I didn't want his apology. I cried and searched.

I prayed for her safe return. Then one morning two days later, my uncle left after breakfast. An hour later he was home, Cindy in his arms.

"She'd been picked up by the pound. I thought I'd check, and there she was," he said. "Must have pulled her collar off somewhere."

Mom let me keep her beside me all night. I hugged her and told her about everything I'd done since she'd been gone. She licked my hand and listened.

She wouldn't leave my side for two days. She limped a bit, though we couldn't find anything wrong. But she was home.

My uncle felt bad and offered to buy me another dog to keep Cindy company outside. I knew he and my aunt were having a hard time. They didn't have much money. I wanted to hate him forever, but I knew he needed us.

One day I came home and found my uncle sitting with Cindy in his lap. He was talking to her. I listened and wondered how long he'd been telling her his troubles. I guess he was smarter than I thought. Cindy stared at him, looking into his face as she'd always done with me when I talked to her.

I watched them for a while. I thought that maybe Cindy and I could give him another chance.

"Want to feed her?" I asked.

He nodded. I gave him the box of her favorite treats. He fed her and stroked her small head.

"She's a good listener," he said.

I smiled. I already knew that. I guess if Cindy forgave him, I could too.

In Her Golden Eyes

Diane Nichols

My six-year-old daughter held on to my hand as we walked through the maze of dog kennels. She loved the furry faces, but the loud barking hurt her ears. I had to shout just to be heard over the commotion.

"Do you see one you think your sister would like for her thirteenth birthday?" I scanned each cage, wincing at the needy brown eyes staring back at me from each one. A neediness for love and belonging. For security and a happy home. Things the girls and I also hungered for since their father and I divorced. In a way, we were just as lost as the souls in these kennels, with a heartbreak I doubted would ever heal.

"I like the little one," she said, pointing to a chubby puppy that wagged its tail so hard it practically fell over. "Can we play with it? Do you think they would let us?"

"I don't see why not."

One of the shelter volunteers allowed us to take the puppy out back in the play yard to see if we were a compatible match. At first Mariah loved to watch him scamper around, but soon he began a fit of biting. The sharp little teeth were a bit much for her to take, and I could tell bringing this one home wouldn't work well.

"Did you see our new arrival?" the volunteer asked. His hair was dyed a funny purplish color and his chin was pierced with a silver ball, but otherwise he was a very charming young man who had an obvious love for animals. He quickly put the puppy back in the kennel with his siblings and led us to another cage where three other puppies were sleeping. They were the size of small bear cubs and had beautiful fur. I could tell right away they were very special.

"What kind are they? A shepherd mix?" I asked, stooping down to take a closer look.

The boy shook his head. "Actually, they're half wolf and half chow. I've never seen such an awesome combination. I took one of the puppies home myself, and he's so smart. He hasn't even been housebroken, but he already knows to go to the bathroom outside. These dogs are going to be beautiful when they grow up."

This was incredible, because Vanessa had always had a passion for wolves, even when she was a very small child. Her bedroom was decorated with statues and posters of them. She had wolf writing paper and silver wolf earrings. Even the blanket on her bed had a design of a majestic wolf tossing its head back and howling at the moon. My heart quickened as the pup in the middle suddenly yawned and looked up at us. She was breathtaking, with thick tan fur, oversized paws, and silvery-black wolf markings on her face. Her eyes struck me the most. They were so gentle and sweet, as golden as her fur. Something told me that this was the one.

Everything the young kennel worker said proved to be true once we got the puppy home. She was cautious

and polite in her new surroundings, never once having an accident on the carpet or the kitchen floor. Instead, she simply seemed thankful for the attention. Mariah hugged her over and over, begging to pick out a name. "We have to wait. Vanessa will be home from school soon, and then we can surprise her with the puppy. Since it's her birthday surprise, it wouldn't be right to name the dog without her."

"Do you think Vanessa will let me help take care of her? After all, I loved her first." Mariah stroked the puppy's shining fur. They made a good team already.

"I'm sure she will." I smiled, wishing her father could be a part of this. It wasn't right that he would miss Vanessa's birthday. Then again, having our marriage crumble around us meant we all missed out. Nobody was the winner.

It seemed forever until Vanessa got out of school, but once she did, we were ready for her. The puppy was hidden on the back porch with a huge sign that Mariah and I decorated with scented markers. It said, "Happy Birthday, Vanessa . . . open the door for your surprise! Love and kisses . . . Mommy and Mariah."

As long as I live, I'll never forget Vanessa's face when she first locked eyes with her very own wolf puppy. It almost made the pain of the last several months disappear. Seeing her smile like that erased all the tears.

"What should we name her?" I asked, beaming as the girls hugged their new friend. "It should be something special. Something beautiful . . . just like her."

Mariah voted for Max, until I told her that was a boy's name. I thought of Sierra, but both girls had a hard time pronouncing it right. Then Vanessa came up with just the right name that fit as perfectly as a hand in glove.

"Cheyenne," she said, gazing into those amazing gold eyes. "Why don't we call her Cheyenne?"

In the coming days Cheyenne accomplished exactly what I was hoping for. Instead of the children feeling homesick for Ohio, since we had moved to Florida to be near my family, they spent time playing with their new puppy. Instead of feeling depressed over missing their daddy, they romped and laughed for hours, playing ball and running around the yard with our new family member. This wonderful wolf pup was helping to fill the void. It gave me hope that the children would handle this very difficult transition a bit better. If only something would help me do the same.

Becoming a single parent after thirteen years of marriage was absolutely terrifying. Suddenly I was alone with two children and a world of heartache. Not only was I hurting over all of my broken dreams, but I was also very worried about finances. I was a freelance writer who didn't make enough to support a family, and I didn't feel as if I had enough energy to support the children emotionally. After watching my marriage fail and my family break apart, I felt as if I had died inside. I went through the motions. I smiled and functioned. I put one foot in front of the other, but it all seemed like a charade. What my soul craved was to crawl into a dark hole somewhere and never have to come out again. If it weren't for the children, I would have.

It didn't take long for the bills to pile up. I tried to hide my fears from the girls, but I knew they sensed my worry. My temper was short, and I was tired all the time. I'm sure they saw my tears. Even Cheyenne sensed that I needed some TLC and curled up beside me at night while I slept.

"Mommy? Are you okay?" Mariah gaped at me during dinner one evening, seeing that I hadn't touched a bite.

I blinked back at her, startled. I had gotten lost in my thoughts. I had been daydreaming about the days when our family meals were happy and their daddy sat at the head of the table. His empty chair now sat to the right of me.

I nodded. "I'm fine, sweetheart. Just eat your food."

She poked at her meatloaf. "But I don't like it."

Vanessa cast her a warning look. She knew how fragile I was. "Mariah, just eat it. Mom worked hard to make us a good dinner."

Simple things like that momentary encounter would often send me running to my room in tears. I wanted to be strong. I wanted to show the children that I was fine and they didn't have to worry. I wanted to be their rock, but I kept falling apart. I ached inside for the life we once had and how safe I used to feel. How was I going to hold us up on my own? How would I ever find the strength to be a single mother? They needed both parents, and I needed a loving husband. Now it was just the three of us, living on government assistance in a neighborhood where we had to worry about our lawn mower being stolen. This wasn't how it was supposed to turn out. My anger began to swallow me whole.

Canine Genealogy

In one sense it's easy—all dogs, no matter what breed or size or appearance, descend from wolves. It's kind of hard to believe that Bubba the pit bull and Charlene the Chihuahua come from the very same family in the beginning, but they do; they, like all dogs, descend from the wolf.

Wolves, being pack animals, were naturals to become our pet dogs. Humans were taming wolves thousands of years ago because they shared compatible lifestyles with them. Both wolves and humans survive by group cooperation, both are playful, and both enjoy one another's company. Over many thousands of years, selective breeding created the best dog for the place and people.

On a hot July afternoon, things took a horrible turn. The children played in the backyard with Cheyenne while I went down the street to visit my parents. We were fortunate enough to live within walking distance, but this day I drove. At least the girls had their grandparents in their lives. But as I got back home and pulled into the driveway, a pickup truck came driving down our street. I got out of my car, keys in hand, and saw Cheyenne run past me in a blur.

"Cheyenne!" I called out. "No! Get back here!" But it was too late. She chased after the truck and caught up to the front tires. The next thing I saw was her body flipping up in the air before landing on the side of the road. She was limp, with a crimson stream of blood running from her mouth. Those golden eyes looked blank and lifeless.

I vaguely remember the children running over. Vanessa was screaming as Mariah clutched onto me and sobbed. My body went numb. It had all happened so fast. The driver of the truck didn't even stop to make sure Cheyenne was all right.

"Oh, God . . . no, please . . . not Cheyenne! This can't be happening." Vanessa's frantic cries filled the air.

My shaking hand gently stroked Cheyenne's side. I expected to have to tell the children that God had taken her up to heaven, but then my breath caught. To my amazement, her heart was still beating. It was faint and fading, but she was hanging on.

"She's still alive," I exclaimed. "We've got to get her to the vet. Mariah, go in the house and get a blanket. Vanessa, help me carry Cheyenne and put her in the backseat of the car. We don't have much time, girls. Please, hurry! We've got to go now!"

Luckily, the vet was still open, and they took her right in. I kept watching Cheyenne's side, willing her to keep breathing as Dr. Chatham laid her on the examining table. Mariah clung to my pant leg in fear as Vanessa hovered by the table, spilling tears and telling Cheyenne that she'd be all right. I remember looking at the dog's still body and the way her eyes rolled back as if seeing nothing. I saw the blood all over our clothes. My stomach pitched as I forced some deep breaths. *Please, God . . . don't let her die. We need her too much. . . . Don't make the children lose another family member they love.*

Dr. Chatham checked her over, including giving special attention to her left front leg, which had a long, deep scrape on it. He then tracked the source of her massive bleeding to a broken blood vessel in her nose. After listening to her heart and carefully feeling for broken bones, he gave us the news that I had been afraid to hope for: our precious Cheyenne was going to be okay. Once she recovered from the shock, she should mend just fine.

"The front leg appears to be the worst of her injuries," he said, pinching between her toes with a silver clamp. "She has no response when I do this. The leg isn't broken, but the nerves have been damaged, and she doesn't have any feeling. Sometimes the damage repairs itself so the dog can use its leg again, but other times the paralysis is permanent and requires amputation. We'll hope for the best. Bring Cheyenne back in six weeks for a recheck. We'll see how her leg is doing by then."

We felt blessed to still have our beloved pet after coming so close to losing her, but watching her limp with her lifeless front leg was difficult. Even as weeks passed by, she had no recovery of movement. She'd hop along, dragging her paw on the ground until it was raw and bleeding. I kept praying that God would give us a miracle and heal her, but I was beginning to think that God had left me along with my husband.

"What are we going to do, Mom?" Vanessa ran a loving hand over Cheyenne's fur as the dog slept next to her on the couch. "I don't want the vet to have to take her leg off. She'll never be happy like that."

Tears blurred my vision as I stared at the pup that had brought so much joy back into my children's life. I couldn't understand why this had to happen. Was everything going to be a heartache from now on? My muscles ached with a weariness that I had never known. I had forgotten what it felt like to smile.

"We have to do what Dr. Chatham thinks is best," I answered, choosing my words carefully. "If he feels that Cheyenne's leg will never recover, we'll have to agree to the surgery."

Vanessa choked back her pain. All she could do was brush back a tear and nod. I felt so helpless. How much heartbreak could a child handle? Why couldn't I make it go away?

On the day of Cheyenne's surgery, Vanessa wanted to stay home from school, but I assured her we wouldn't hear any news until the afternoon. It was best if she kept busy and was distracted with her friends. I promised her that I'd call her if I heard anything from the vet any sooner. Mariah and I passed the hours by cleaning the house and watching videos. She'd giggle at the cartoon characters while my thoughts drifted back to Cheyenne. All I could do was worry and wonder how she'd cope without her front leg.

Before long Vanessa was home, and then it was time to pick up Cheyenne. We all piled into the car with eager hearts, hoping and praying that everything was okay. According to the vet technician who called me once the procedure was over, Cheyenne had come through with flying colors.

"She'll be very wobbly and groggy for the rest of the night," the technician told us once we arrived at the clinic. "The anesthesia will take a while to wear off, and she'll need her pain medication for the next few days. She's going to be very uncomfortable for a while, but pretty soon she'll be able to walk again."

Nothing had prepared us for what we would see once we made our way back to the kennels. In the bottom cage, Cheyenne lay panting and blinking sleepy eyes, the entire right side of her body shaved clean from her stomach to her neck. A huge white bandage was wrapped around her shoulder area where her leg used to be. A plastic tube was also taped to the area to help the surgical site drain. She looked totally miserable.

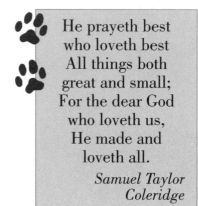

He prayeth best
who loveth best
All things both
great and small;
For the dear God
who loveth us,
He made and
loveth all.

*Samuel Taylor
Coleridge*

Tears slid from my eyes as I saw Cheyenne's tail give a faint wag. She recognized her family even in her foggy state and was obviously happy to see us. Vanessa bent down and began talking to her. She told her we had come to take her home. The sound of her voice made Cheyenne try to stand up, but she immediately fell over against the wall with a yelp.

"She'll need a lot of help walking and standing," said the technician, opening the door to the cage. "For the next few days, you'll need to hold her up and help her to get around. She'll eventually get stronger and adapt to the use of three legs. You'd be surprised how well dogs get around after an amputation. She'll be able to do just about everything she used to do, after she heals."

I hung on to those words during that first night of Cheyenne's long recovery. As she moaned in agony and lay on her side, unable to move, I kept trying to picture her as she used to be: running, playing, jumping up on the bed to snuggle down and sleep next to me. I thought about how she'd go to her toy basket and choose her favorite stuffed animal to plop in our laps so we'd play tug-of-war with her. I felt frightened and uncertain, wondering how she would ever be that same carefree pup again. In a way I understood the kind of trauma she was going through. One day you're happy, and the next you're in a world of pain.

Vanessa and I slept on the floor with Cheyenne for the first few nights. We'd keep watch, try to comfort her, give her pain pills, and feed her vanilla ice cream from a spoon. It was the only thing that seemed to taste good to her. She would lap at it until she was full, then lay her head back down on the floor and doze. Every few hours Vanessa and I carried her outside to the yard and helped her stand so she could go to the bathroom. We were exhausted, but nothing was more important than Cheyenne coming back to us . . . even if she would never be the same again.

Come Monday I had to take care of her myself when Vanessa went to school. Mariah kept busy with her coloring books and TV while I hovered over Cheyenne. I changed her bandages and made sure she wasn't trying to bite at them. I stroked her head and told her how strong she was. Seeing her so miserable and watching the blood ooze from her drainage tube kept breaking my heart over and over again. I missed her sweet eyes looking at me with love instead of so much suffering. Just as I couldn't take away my children's pain since the divorce, I couldn't erase Cheyenne's either. I felt like I couldn't do anything at all except stand by and watch everything crumble.

"You're a survivor," I whispered in Cheyenne's ear as she closed her sleepy eyes. "You can do this. You're a strong girl. We need you, so you have to get better. Those children are depending on you, so please . . . don't give up. Fight and get through this."

As I said those words to her, something struck me deep inside. The same thing I was saying to her, I knew was true for myself. Life had been a nightmare since the divorce, and the pain went so deep that I wanted to curl up and die. I didn't see myself as able to stand on my own. I felt so broken and defeated.

But weren't the children depending on me too? Didn't I have to fight and get through this? What was the alternative? Was I really going to show my daughters that we were ruined and would never be okay again? Tears ran down my cheeks as I lay my face against Cheyenne's muzzle. It was so soft, and her breaths fanned my skin—breaths that reminded me how precious life is.

"I love you," I said as my heart welled with new-found hope that we could make it together. "I'll make a deal with you, girl. If you fight and get through this, I'll fight my way back too. We'll learn how to walk on our own together."

From that day on, I sensed a change in Cheyenne and in me. We began to blossom like two wilted flowers coming back to life. She looked more alert and comfortable, daring to take her first steps, while I started crying less and smiling more. A healing was beginning to take place, and it felt so very good. Instead of dwelling on the past, I felt ready to plan a future. I saw myself as able instead of shattered, lost, and frightened. One day at a time, one step at a time, Cheyenne and I were making it together.

"Look, Mom! She's doing it! Cheyenne's walking on her own!" Vanessa pointed as Cheyenne wandered about the yard one week later. She managed just fine with the front leg missing. In fact, she didn't seem to miss it much at all.

I smiled, feeling the warmth of the sun on my face. The world looked colorful and bright again. "Yes, isn't she amazing? Next thing you know, she'll be chasing butterflies again."

Mariah laughed. "Just like her old self."

I thought about that a moment and had to disagree. "Actually, sweetheart . . . I think Cheyenne's going to be better than she used to be. She'll be stronger because she's a survivor now. Just like us . . . better than ever."

And in that instant, Cheyenne stopped and looked at me. The gleam was back in those golden eyes. It was as if God had brought us together so we could help one another through our darkest hours. Two survivors with a new life to look forward to, one precious step at a time.

A Dog Named Blue
Hilary Walker

Blue chose me. I adored him from the start and was thrilled when he made it clear to his previous owner that he wanted to go home with me that day.

We'd moved to England from Italy, but my husband still worked on the Continent. Glen would fly over whenever possible on weekends, but mostly I was alone with our three-year-old son in a centuries-old Cotswold stone house in the middle of twenty-six acres. I did not enjoy my dark walk to the stables for the nightly check on our four horses.

I decided a big dog was in order—a fierce-looking pet. Scouring the ads, I saw a couple of bullmastiffs for sale and drove over to see them. They rushed to the wire fencing of their outdoor kennels with "kill" written all over their faces. These were no pets!

In despair I reread the paper and spotted a fifteen-month-old Great Dane looking for a new home. All I knew about the breed was that it's huge. Curiosity made me dial the number.

Soon I was standing in front of a house the size of a postage stamp, with an even smaller garden, in a crowded neighborhood. *What ever possessed the owners to buy such a large dog?* I mused while ringing the front bell. On the other side of the bottled glass door loomed a massive, dark form with a man in tow, who opened the door. Next to his owner stood a very polite, huge Great Dane who looked at me inquiringly. Three feet at his shoulder, he was dark gray with a white bib and two white paws. He didn't make a sound.

When I put out my hand to stroke his head, the dog graciously allowed me to touch him. As I needed to know how dog and boy would get on, I'd brought my son with me. Ross fearlessly copied his mother, instinctively trusting the animal whose big black nose pushed into the little hand stretching high to touch him.

"Come in," said the man, holding out his hand. "The name's John Jones."

"I'm Hilary Walker, and this is my son, Ross."

We shook hands and followed him into his diminutive sitting room, where Ross and I sat on the sofa and he sat opposite us in an armchair.

"What's his name?" I asked, pointing to the gentle monster.

"Smoky," he replied, then asked anxiously, "What kind of dog are you looking for?"

He fondled the animal's large gray ears as its chiseled head leaned into the arms of his seat. When I told him, he asked, "You just don't want a guard dog, then?"

"No," I reassured him, "I want a pet who *looks* like a guard dog."

John was reassured. Then another thought worried him.

"Do you have enough room for him to live in the house with you? I really hate to let him go, but we're not allowed pets here. And anyway, this house is too small for him."

"Our house is pretty big, and we have twenty-six acres for him to run around in," I explained.

John smiled. "Sounds ideal. But could I check your property before you take Smoky?"

"Of course," I replied.

Then Smoky did something extraordinary. He moved away from John's chair, padded on huge paws over to mine, and turned around to plant his very substantial rear end in my lap, confident I'd be flattered. I was! Pleased as anything at his showing such trust and acceptance of a stranger, I continued talking as if nothing had happened and stroked the tall, broad back of the heavy dog sitting coolly on my legs. I had to peer around him to maintain eye contact with his owner. When I stroked the dog's face, he pressed his wide muzzle into my palm. *You're okay,* he seemed to say. Ross leaned across and cuddled the huge torso. Smoky turned his head in benevolent approval: *You're a good kid.*

Tears formed in John's eyes as he related how well the dog played with his little daughter and how loath he was to part with him. The dog's next home *had* to be a good one. I learned that Smoky's particular color was called blue. I learned that Great Danes have small hearts for the size of their body and therefore a short life expectancy—usually six to seven years. Overexercise can easily twist their intestines, but they do need a lot of room for wagging their never-ending tails. I was soon to learn that Great Danes knock a lot of stuff off coffee tables and shelves and have heads the ideal height for circling sharklike around the dinner table, looking for scraps.

Suddenly John said, "Look, I can

see the dog likes you, and I saw your Range Rover outside, so I believe you've enough space for a big dog. Why don't you take him now?"

"Are you sure?" I could see how hard this was for him.

"Yes."

I wrote a check for an obscene amount of money (these big pups cost a lot), and Ross beamed at me. After a good-bye stroke from John, Smoky happily jumped into the very back of the Range Rover. I buckled Ross up in the rear passenger seat and drove off, after assuring John he could check on us anytime. A forlorn man looked out of the tiny home from which he'd released a beloved pet.

Two seconds into our trip, Smoky decided the back of the car wasn't his scene and gave an enormous leap over to sit next to Ross. This was a big improvement, the cheeky dog clearly thought as he leaned across my son and stuck his bull-sized head out the window.

I watched the huge nose and fluttering ears in my side mirror. *What have I done?* I asked myself in horror. *Suppose this animal kills my son? What kind of irresponsible parent am I?* But Ross thought it was funny. He giggled at the furry bulk looming over him, and I stopped fretting.

When we got home I let Smoky out, somehow knowing he wouldn't run off. After one look at our grass fields, he gave a joyous yelp and bounded off to race around in humungous circles. He was a terrifying sight: his huge jowls flapped up and down

71

with the lumbering movement of his body to reveal long, pointed fangs. When he'd exhausted himself and I was remembering John's warning about knotted intestines, he lunged at me in gratitude for bringing him here and knocked me over. It was a great start to our relationship and a reminder to have him neutered as soon as possible.

Another change I made to him was his name. He was definitely a smoky color, but "Smoky" was too weak for a dog as strong as I'd just found out he was. Since his color was "blue," he became "Smoky Blue," which quickly shortened to "Blue."

It then occurred to me that my pseudo–guard dog hadn't once barked. How was he going to ward off would-be burglars? Maybe that was the real reason his owner had sold him. But it was too late now—I was in love, and the dog was staying.

Blue needed to meet the horses, who would be a big part of his life. He was almost a year and a half old and unfamiliar with animals larger than himself, so I wondered how this meeting would go. He followed Ross and me up to the barn where four equine heads poked over their doors to inspect the newcomer.

If I'd been concerned he couldn't bark, I needn't worry anymore. He nearly brought down the barn with the reverberations! He had no idea what to make of the horses and appeared dreadfully threatened. Trouble was, there were too many of them for him to know which head to bark at first. So he stayed at the far end of the aisle to let them *all* know that he had a very loud voice.

The horses blinked in surprise: who did he think he was? Did he really hope they'd be scared? Forget it! Soon they went back to munching their hay, and I took Blue back outside to recover from the shock to his ego.

It took him awhile to get used to the large equines, but when he did, he thoroughly enjoyed romping around the countryside with me whenever I went on a trail ride. His big party trick was to rush down the drive ahead of me as I rode home and hide behind a bush. He'd leap out in front of the horse I was riding and frighten it. The horses never got used to it; that made Blue's day.

Having now discovered that he could bark without being reprimanded, Blue would practice early every morning. He'd sit in the pasture like a monarch and echo across the valley to rouse lazy stragglers in the neighboring village. Eventually I had to ask him for more considerate timing and frequency, and he duly obliged.

Ross's formal English education began the following fall when he was four. His school was on rugged open land called Minchinhampton Common. I'd take Blue with me in the afternoons to fetch Ross, and all three of us would go for a walk. The September weather was warm and the blackberry bushes full of fruit. After picking copious amounts, we sat on a rustic bench picnicking together while

Blue rummaged among the interesting smells of local wildlife.

One afternoon in late autumn, we set off across the common toward a sun slung low in the red-streaked sky. Ross and Blue walked side by side (the Great Dane never needed a leash) while I followed behind, watching the little boy whose head barely rose above the big dog's withers as they strode along in companionable silence. We were climbing a hill, and the line of its crest looked like the start of the sky. Ross turned back and shouted to me with a big grin, "Look, Mummy! Blue and I are walking to the edge of the world!"

The reason a dog has so many friends is that he wags his tail instead of his tongue.

Anonymous

He'd described the scene exactly. I stood still and drank in the beauty of it.

Boy and dog were now on the brow of the hillock, etched against the sky with long shadows falling behind them. The sunset's wide orange and crimson veins flowed slowly across the horizon, softly lighting a path for the intrepid adventurers setting out to conquer earth before nightfall.

I shall never forget that beautiful tableau, a magic moment suspended in time, given to me by the loving Great Dane. Thanks to him, my fast-growing son is engraved forever on my mind as an innocent four-year-old enjoying the company of his canine buddy, whom he trusted completely and who was his constant playmate through the ups and downs of that first year at school.

Blue was to experience much excitement and give us many wonderful memories. He was only three years old when crippling arthritis took away the fun in his life, forcing my difficult yet necessary decision to end his suffering.

I wanted him to die peacefully in the home where he was so loved. When the vet came, Blue was snuggled down on a blanket in his favorite place next to the white Aga oven in the kitchen. His tummy was warm with a grand last supper of steak and rice, and the huge animal gave a long sigh as the swift injection freed his soul from his pain-racked body. He left behind a legacy of love and loyalty and the enduring gift to my son of a boyhood spent together on the common, lit by the gloaming.

In the corner of an English field lies a beautiful blue Great Dane with the biggest heart God ever gave a dog.

Puppy Love

Callie Smith Grant

When I was five years old, my parents were going through a divorce. Needless to say, it was not pleasant.

My grandmother lived with us and took care of me while my mother worked outside the home for the first time. And while that provided some stability, Grandma used a wheelchair, which confined her to one area of the house. My older sister coped with the changes afoot in her own way: by staying away from the house as much as possible. We lived in the farmland, and I had very few playmates. I often found myself more or less alone.

I loved school and would have preferred to be there all day. But kindergarten was a half day, and I was home by noon. I wanted my mother to be there waiting for me, but she was working. Dad had moved out. I didn't understand any of these changes. I didn't receive a lot of attention then; the grown-ups had other things on their minds.

That spring our wirehaired terrier, Muggs, gave birth to a litter of puppies who were fathered by the neighboring beagle. This was exciting stuff! Each day when I came home from school, the first thing I would do was change into my outdoor clothes. I'd yell to Grandma that I'd be right back for lunch, and then I'd hurry outside to the most wonderful thing.

Mama Muggs and her six puppies lived in the stone smokehouse behind the house, and it had a gothic-looking wooden door on it. When I opened the creaky door, the noon light would edge across the dirt floor, and then I could see all those little tails inside start to wag. I could hear the yipping and snorting and the generally happy sounds puppies make.

I would turn and quickly drop to the ground. I'd lie straight on my stomach and cover the sides of my face with my hands. All those little guys would scamper outside and crawl all over me and lick whatever skin they could find. They'd sniff and yip and carry on and try to get to my face with their little wet noses. They'd chew on my long braids. They especially loved licking my ears. They didn't romp away; they stayed right with me, crawling all over me while I giggled. It made me so happy I forgot my family troubles for a while every day.

I am much older now, and I have the stresses all adults have. I understand these many years later the value of focusing attention on something good during times of stress. Professionals confirm what animal lovers already know—that pets can provide comfort and stability to their guardians. Even other people's pets can soothe people in hospitals, rest homes, and war zones.

Sometimes when I need to calm myself, I pull inside and go back to that stone smokehouse. I remember the anticipation of opening the creaky door. I remember dropping to the good dark earth, then the feeling of being greeted by squirming puppies with wet noses. I still recall the pleasure of those puppy kisses. And inside I giggle.

A Shepherd

Bonnie Leon

Our three kids scrambled out of the car and ran toward a collection of yellow, wriggling, tail-wagging pups. Our friends had adopted a very pregnant stray yellow lab weeks before. Now they had a litter needing homes. We'd decided to be one of the adoptive families. However, we had guidelines: the adoptee would be female (no leg-lifting allowed on our property), couldn't be too large, and mustn't be overly rambunctious.

In the yard, laughter and squeals of delight emerged from our brood of kids, who were surrounded by wet noses and licking tongues. Although we'd decided deliberation and caution should be displayed in making a choice, my husband and I were soon drawn into the enchantment of eager puppies.

Almost immediately we noticed a large, white male. "No," we told ourselves. "No males, and he's too big."

Then our son and the white puppy found each other. My husband and I watched as the two made an instant connection. We knew he belonged with us. Yes, he was the biggest of the pups, and yes, he was male, and yes, he had more energy than any self-respecting dog ought to have, but . . . he belonged to us. This fluffy white bundle—who looked very much like a polar bear cub—and the Leon family were a match.

Weeks and then months followed, and Ben (better known as Benny) adhered himself to our hearts and to one heart in particular. Our son Paul and Benny were comrades. Benny made the choice, really—Paul became Benny's boy.

As the two grew older, they remained partners. They did everything together—hiking through the forest, mountain biking, and camping. They even built igloos together. Well, actually Benny watched while Paul did the building. I have a picture in my mind of Benny sitting atop a nearly melted igloo. It was his patch of cold ground, and he'd guard his scrap of white until it completely melted.

Paul wasn't Benny's only friend; he was just his best friend. All the Leons mattered to him, and we loved him in return.

Ben grew and grew and grew. At his prime he weighed 115 pounds. He had a heavy white coat and a broad chest. He always held his wide head up proudly, meeting the world with poise and dignity. He was never rude—he never chewed up things that didn't belong to him; he never destroyed our plants or our gardens. I don't think he had a single accident indoors. He was the perfect dog.

He did guard. I noticed right off that he always seemed to be on watch. I didn't worry about him biting one of our friends, but I knew he would fend off anyone who didn't belong. He seemed to have a sixth sense about that sort of thing. Rightly so, because as it turns out, Benny was half Kuvasz, which is a Belgian breed used to guard sheep. A Kuvasz lives among the flock. He doesn't bully them or herd them; he simply guards, protecting the sheep from predators.

That's how Benny was with us. We were his flock. He'd happily accept our friends, sometimes showing too much affection. After all, a 115-pound dog leaning against your leg can be a bit much for some. He loved to play. When he was in a mood for fun, we had need for caution. A fast-moving, frolicking mass of white could easily knock you off your feet. We learned this by experience . . . more than once.

By the time Ben was full grown, he'd taken on the distinct role of protector. I never worried about our children when they hiked in the forest or enjoyed overnight campouts as long as Benny was with them. I had no doubt that he would watch over my flock. The kids understood this too.

They loved sleeping out, and Ben always lay beside them. Throughout the night he'd stay close. Often I'd

Anthropomorphize, Anyone?

This term refers to our tendency to attribute human characteristics and urges to animals. We pet lovers especially tend to do this with our dogs, and to some extent that's fine in that it helps us connect with our dog. But we're really better off realizing we are very different from each other even though we share some characteristics that are similar. Rather than expecting our dogs to think and behave like humans, we would do well to try to think like a dog when dealing with our pet. A misbehaving dog, for example, does not usually have an agenda of wanting to get on our last nerve. Rover lives with internal urges that are completely animal, not human, and our realizing this doesn't need to make Rover any less lovable.

peek out to see if all was well, and there he'd be, either lying quietly among them or sitting on his haunches and looking out into the darkness, watching and listening. I would return to my bed knowing my children were being looked after.

We felt peace in Ben's presence. I never doubted his loyalty or his courage, and I knew that if called upon, he would offer his life. One day it dawned on me that he was a living (if unorthodox) example of my heavenly Father—always caring, always watching, willing to make the ultimate sacrifice.

The years passed and our children grew up and left home. Benny stayed behind with my husband and me. Even when Ben grew old, he never relinquished his position as protector. All those years he and our UPS man remained at odds. Maybe it was the uniform; we never knew—but rarely did the UPS man step inside our fenced yard.

Ben remained handsome until his thirteenth year. Not until then did we see his health decline. Still, he would perk up when our son Paul or one of our daughters came for a visit, and he could still leap, ears flapping, at mealtime. And yet we knew that soon he would leave us. It was only a matter of time.

And the day came.

We found him lying in a thatch of deep, green grass. He'd found the perfect place—sweet-smelling, cool, and damp. He looked like he was asleep, his big head resting on his paws. There was a sense of serenity about him. He'd done what he'd been called to do; his life's work had been fulfilled. I'll never know who or what may have been put off by his presence. I do know he was always on duty, and our family remained safe through the years.

Some may say he was "just" a dog. To us, he was more. He was family, and he was a perfect picture of love, honor, and courage.

"Greater love has no one than this, that he lay down his life for his friends" (see John 15:13 NIV). Benny did just that. Every day he lived for us.

She Knew

Twila Bennett

My father-in-law was the friendliest man you'd ever meet. He had a sparkle in his eyes that could light up a room. He had a laugh that helped get you started. He was stubborn. He loved steak. He adored his grandchildren, and his dogs were his babies. Cruises were his dream vacation. He was married and had two sons. He actually enjoyed mowing the lawn. Hard work never bothered him. He loved driving his Jeep.

He was suddenly stricken with cancer at age fifty-four.

His cancer was incurable.

Oh, everyone gave it their best shot. He went to smart doctors who seemed to know what they were talking about (most days). He went to big cities to get chemo treatments and came home to the country to let them attack his body.

He suffered in silence on a couch during the day, his dogs at his side, while he pondered what life had thrown at him and wished to God it hadn't happened to him.

The older dog became sick, and it broke his heart. The family pondered the similarities in their illnesses and wondered at the connectedness of this dog and her man.

He tried to act as if nothing was wrong when family and friends came to visit. But they could see it in his eyes. This battle was going to be hard on him. They didn't speak it, but they wondered in quiet whispers far away from him if he would make it.

And then one day, a beautiful August day, he laughed again. Strength came to him in ways that were unexplainable. Perhaps it was the joy in being with his son outside in a lawn chair on that sunny morning. Or maybe it was the hug from a grandson who sat on his lap. Maybe it was a friend dropping by.

A moment frozen in time. The sunlight on his face, a chuckle, a glance.

But that evening the cancer took over. He was losing, and everyone knew it. He was rushed to the hospital with those he loved at his side.

I waited at the house in the country with my son and the one little dog that was, truth be told, his favorite. This dog had always needed him, you see. She had been born with a cleft palate and had seizures for which she took expensive medicine. She had severe eye problems that were impossible to correct. But there was no way that the man would have her put to sleep. She was a tiny thing, with a big attitude to boot. He loved her with all his heart, and she knew it.

It was a long night for me, not being able to be with the rest of the family but somehow all the while sitting with them in that hospital room from afar. Praying for them. Wanting it to just all be over. Wanting the present to move forward. Hurting.

As the night dragged into day, I waited. There was no sunshine that morning as I puttered around the house.

When the phone rang, I knew. I took the phone outside, away from the prying eyes of a child who had never known pain. And I brought along the little dog to somehow explain to her afterward that the love of her life was gone. I knew that my father-in-law would have wanted it that way.

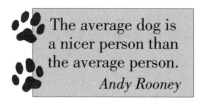

The average dog is a nicer person than the average person.

Andy Rooney

My husband, his son, choked out amidst sobs, "He's gone." Two words that are dreaded more than any words in the human language. Words that go straight to the gut. The earth shifts on its axis and life moves on.

We talked of details, of the last moments, of his mother, of this and that. And as I looked up toward the sky with tears in my eyes, the sun shone. Brilliantly. Joyously. So bright it hurt my eyes. A wind began blowing around me and the dog and the trees at the country house with a bounce and lightness that left me speechless.

And the dog began howling, over and over again, nose to the sky and to the wind. She strained her blind eyes to see.

But I saw. She was saying good-bye to her soul mate. She knew.

Nikki

Kristi Hemingway

earing the bell ring, I looked up to see Linda
wrestling a big cardboard box through the
door. She was the wife of my summer boss,
and she often dropped by just to chat.

"Have I got a deal for you," she yelled as she bumped
her way through the Twinkies and Cheetos. Hoisting
the box onto the kitchen counter, she smiled widely.
"Free for the taking!"

I peered over the edge at what looked—and
smelled—like an old coat from the thrift store reject
pile, but then the mound of black fur began to squirm
and squeak. Leaning closer, I recognized small black
noses, tiny silken ears, and little twitching paws: a box
of puppies. Squealing, I dove in with the delight of a
toddler with chocolate ice cream. Nuzzling three at a
time, I chose the smallest, pledging lifelong love and
care without a single nanosecond of reflection.

Reflection probably would have been wise.

"Who is going to care for her while you're at work?" Mom's hands were planted on her hips, and her eyebrows were raised in that pinched way over her blazing blue eyes. "And where in the world is she going to live in three weeks when you leave for school?"

"Well, I was kind of thinking she could stay with you until . . . well, until I'm done with—"

"With *us*?" she interrupted, pitch rising. "You mean in the *new* house?"

Ah yes, the new house. We were all spending the summer crammed into a tiny condominium, awaiting completion of the new house. A dream house, full of new carpet and nice furniture and pristine screens and windows—all untouched by canine paws. This puppy idea was definitely not selling like I had hoped. Perhaps Nikki would do a better job of selling herself. She was contentedly nestled on my chest, making her little puppy wheezes and coos as I kneaded one of her satin paws between my fingers.

"But, Mom, look at her. She's soooo sweet. She's irresistible."

"Of course she's irresistible. All puppies are irresistible. But you have three *years* of college left and who knows what after that. There's just no way this can be your dog, and she's *not* going to be mine. Period. I'm sorry, but you'd better start making some phone calls." Mom's resolve was mildly sympathetic but firm.

My grandmothers came immediately to mind. They were both alone—one widowed and one divorced. I felt that either of them would be a perfect fit, but Dad disagreed. "You're crazy. Neither of your grandmothers needs the hassle of a puppy, of all things. I can save you the trouble of those two phone calls right now."

It couldn't hurt to try. Grandma Bea, regaining composure from a snort that turned to a coughing bout, informed me that she was "plenty" content with her parakeet. Grandma Marjorie didn't have a parakeet and therefore jumped straight to flat refusal. "Oh my goodness! Heavens no! You're not serious, Kristi."

For two weeks I prayed. I was determined to keep Nikki in the family. She needed us, and somehow I knew that we needed her too. What was the point of giving her to just anyone? I might as well just give her back to Linda. My mother issued her daily questions and warnings.

"Have you been making calls about that dog?" Mom refused to call Nikki by her name. I knew it was a defense mechanism. I had taken Psych 101.

It was my last Friday at work, and on Saturday morning I would be heading two states away for my second year of college. I issued a final tearful plea to my parents at dinner. They were unmoved and sent me sniffling to the telephone to call Linda and tell her I'd be bringing Nikki back tomorrow. Just as I reached for the receiver, it rang. It was Grandma Marjorie.

"If you haven't returned that puppy yet, I've decided that maybe I do need a little company around here after all."

My leaping and screaming finally calmed enough for me to relate the conversation. Mom sat with her eyes sparkling, shaking her head and mumbling sentence fragments of disbelief. "My mother? Not in a million . . . Of course, I should've known with you praying . . . I just can't . . . How? . . . And that's all she said? . . . She certainly needs some companionship, but I . . . my mother . . . Well, I guess God has a plan here. That's the only explanation."

And God did. Nikki, inexplicably shy and skittish, would never have tolerated a big, noisy family. Grand-

ma's quiet, loving company suited her perfectly, and vice versa. My once-fastidious grandmother took to walking around with her dress coated with dog hair and face bathed in dog kisses. Nikki provided years of motivation and structure that kept my grandmother active and alert. She'd say, "That little dog is the one who gets me out of bed in the morning and keeps me on schedule all day. Not sure what I'd do without her."

Grandma was no longer single. She became "Grandma and Nikki," inextricably linked like Calvin and Hobbes or Charlie Brown and Snoopy.

When Grandma Marjorie eventually succumbed to Alzheimer's disease, Nikki remained her link to reality. Grandma would busy her hands in Nikki's fur, reciting to her story after story from the past with detailed accuracy. When the day came for Grandma to have full-time care, Nikki could not accompany her to her new home. They both anticipated their visits with the joy of a puppy and a child, and even when Grandma started confusing all of our names and faces, she always knew her little dog.

Nikki went to live in the new house after all—now fifteen years old. Mom and I often joked about the irony of her ending up with Nikki, but she readily welcomed the comfort that Nikki brought. They grieved together over the slow, piece-by-piece loss of the woman they had known as Mother. Grandma, with more of her life and memories slipping away in a steady stream, one day stopped asking about Nikki.

Nikki had grown deaf and a little blind and spent most of her time under the bed.

I was living in the Netherlands when Mom called one day to tell me that Nikki had died. I spent that afternoon walking in the park, watching people and their dogs, my pockets full of tissues. Mom had been right. Nikki could never have been my dog. I had spent my postcollege years touring with a theater company and then relocated to Europe. But Nikki's life had been determined not by practicality alone—but by a plan. That plan brought years of life, comfort, and joy to a whole family because a homeless puppy and an elderly lady found what they needed in each other.

Bo, the Dancing Dog

Julianne Dwelle

I was forty-five years old and found myself in a predicament.

Never a thin woman in my entire life, I had recently gained a lot more weight. Years of yo-yo dieting had brought my metabolism down to a slow crawl, and then a lengthy thyroid problem packed on a dangerous number of extra pounds. It exhausted me into near immobility. I finally was in successful treatment for the thyroid issue, but it did not produce any weight loss. I would have to get the weight off myself. I was discouraged before I even started.

I knew better than to do something too extreme too quickly. A lifetime of dieting had taught me that quick weight loss was counterproductive in every way—I had learned at least that much. My eating habits actually needed only minor adjustments. The problem was exercise. I hadn't been getting any at all for a couple of years. My illness had kept me even from cleaning my own house or gardening without help.

Now my doctor and I had a chat, and he kept his instructions brief. "You know you have to exercise," he said. "Figure it out."

Before getting sick, I had been an avid walker. For years I had chosen to live in large cities where I wouldn't need a car, and I'd walked everywhere. In addition, during those years I had intentionally chosen third-story apartments in buildings without elevators because I knew climbing stairs was good for me. During several of those years, I also swam daily and took dance lessons weekly.

The day came, however, when for a variety of reasons I had moved to a remote place where I became completely dependent on driving long distances to get anywhere. There were no swimming pools anywhere around me. Nobody was dancing either.

The future, however, was looking brighter. Just being out of bed and moving around enabled me to drop a few pounds right away. But I was clueless as to how to fix the intentional exercise issue. I didn't live in a good place for walking, and I was still weak. One day I found myself actually praying for solutions. Then it came to me out of nowhere: join a gym.

Join a gym? Where did that come from? Growing up, I was a bookworm, and I hated gyms. I hated phys ed class in high school. I hated locker rooms. I hated sports events, despised track and field . . . oh, I could go on and on.

Are They Simply Fun to Have Around?

It's common knowledge that people of all ages fare better emotionally and physically with pets in their lives. Much of that well-being comes from the companionship and unconditional love a pet provides. And some of that well-being may come from the act of caring for one's pet, where our focus is off self and onto the needs of another creature.

Dogs in particular not only are loyal and loving companions but also can provide more care than they actually need. Dogs lead the blind, find the injured, comfort the grieving, warn us of danger, and even sense health problems; for example, some dogs are trained to sense oncoming seizures. Now some dogs can even sniff out when a diabetic's glucose level is dangerously low.

But it occurred to me that maybe the one thing I hated was the very thing that could work for me—a gym. And since I was clueless about what I'd do there, maybe I could hire a personal trainer to help me.

Except I'd never even *met* anyone who was a personal trainer. Did they exist here in the Plains? I got out the phone book. As I suspected, there were no gyms in my entire county. The adjacent county had two gyms listed. Knowing nothing about either of them, I chose the one marginally closer to me—almost thirty miles away, at that—and I called.

A man answered: "Body Building. May I help you?"

Body Building? Oh dear. I had a fleeting vision of shirtless musclemen and women in fuchsia thongs. Nevertheless, I asked to speak to the manager.

"That would be me," he said. "Actually, I'm the owner."

He sounded nice enough. I asked him if his gym had personal trainers.

"I train," he answered.

I took a deep breath. "Can you work with someone who is really overweight and out of shape?"

He didn't hesitate. "Sure."

I noted the lack of hesitation. "What would we do?"

He thought for a moment, then outlined a basic workout and a reasonable schedule. I asked him again if he really felt he could work comfortably with someone who was very overweight.

This time he paused. "Well, I suppose I should have your doctor's written release." Since under the circumstances I knew my doctor would kiss his feet for this, I assured him he'd have it. Then he added, "But I really think you should stop in and meet me and look the place over. Then you can see what we're doing here, and you can decide if this is what you want."

I agreed to it. A couple days later, I showed up at the Body Building, and a nice-looking, solid-bodied man around my age met me at the door. He was Richard, the man on the phone. He looked me straight in the eyes and offered his hand. He was not someone to be afraid of.

And that's when I saw the dog at his feet. A mix of springer spaniel and border collie, he was the kind of dog who seems to be smiling all the time. His coat was black and cinnamon with some beige and white here and there, and he had sort of a plumed tail. Best of all, his feet were covered with long, white hair flaring out from his ankles like bell-bottom cuffs. His ankles reminded me of the ankles on Clydesdale horses.

The dog's name was Bo—short for Bodacious. Later I would learn that sometimes Richard called him Bo-jangles because Bo could dance on his hind legs. And Bo had the most stunning eyes I'd ever seen on a dog— they were the color of caramels, with that wonderful direct eye contact many dogs give. I held my hand out to Bo, palm down. He sniffed my hand and wagged his gorgeous tail. We were friends right away.

Richard had told me the best time to come to the gym when there would be very few people around so that I'd feel more comfortable. Indeed, only one person was working out. And he was not shirtless at all.

As promised, Richard showed me around, and even though I was in street clothes, he insisted I try some of the machines. It was a good move, because I had literally never set foot in a commercial gym before, and I was truly in alien territory. All those machines looked alike. And kind of scary.

Bo stood at attention while Richard and I agreed on a workout and a schedule. I petted the dog before I left, and I felt good about things. The next day I found myself at the gym ready to roll. Some guys were there lifting, but they just gave me a quick nod and went about their routines.

And of course there was Bo. He followed us around, tail wagging, as Richard led me from machine to machine, giving me tips on how to use my muscles and talking me through the reps. Bo seemed very interested and relaxed, watching me with his caramel eyes. But I also could see that he was protective of his territory and of Richard. Whenever someone walked in whose scent he did not know, he could cause quite a racket. That pretty dog could also look mighty intimidating. But on this, my first day in the gym, Bo was very sociable toward me, the stranger.

The final machine at the end of my workout was a stationary bike. Because of some painting and rearranging going on in the gym, the bike was in a room all by itself. The first time I used the stationary bike, I was so weak and uncoordinated from my recent inactivity that Richard had to pick up my feet and place them on the pedals. The first few times he talked me through ten tough minutes of pedaling. After that, he left me alone to work at my own pace on the bike.

But Bo never left me alone in the room. Bo curled right around the base of the bike while I huffed and puffed and sweated. When I was done, he would follow me out of the room. Before long, when I arrived at the gym, Bo would trot outside to meet me right at my car door, his furry mouth smiling, his caramel eyes calm and intelligent. I wasn't the only person he did this with, but I felt special anyway. I would talk to him while I got my gear together and locked my car.

Then Bo would follow me indoors, his tail wagging. Sometimes I gave him a treat, and he would dance on his hind legs for it. Sometimes as I worked out, I would pull off my outer sweatshirt and toss it on the floor, and Bo curled up on that.

One time I wasn't paying attention, and I left my purse on the floor in the open while I worked out in the next room. The gym was busy that morning, and after around twenty minutes, I suddenly realized that I had several hundred dollars in my purse. I hurried to get it.

Bo was curled around my purse, sleeping.

Some years have passed, and I still work out at the gym on a regular basis. Richard still trains me, and we've become very good friends. Bo still meets me at my car. After Bo dances for his treats, he curls up on my jacket while I work out.

Today I am lighter, stronger, and still on my way to better health. I credit Richard for helping me get there. In fact, I believe Richard probably helped save my life . . . with the assistance of Bo, the dancing dog.

And You Think Your Dog's Smart?

Nancy Jo Eckerson

I have always been amazed at pet owners and their insane attitudes toward their animals. I myself had never really owned a pet until recently. I say never *really* because I did find a turtle near the creek one summer and brought it home. I set up a turtle-arium in a wheelbarrow with lots of water, some great climbing rocks, and grass clippings for "Ted" to munch on. The first night of our life together proved to be our last (sigh). Ted jumped ship and took off into the night. I took this as a sign that I was not a natural for pet ownership. I suppose the real blessing here was that he did bail out on me, because they say that people tend to take on the appearance of their pets.

Honestly, I can never relate to the "my pet does ten tricks and I haven't even trained him" types. And people who let their dogs and cats lick them are from another planet. How could that be safe? I mean, you know what else they lick? Ugh.

Another one of my pet peeves—people who talk to their animals as if they're their offspring.

"Come to Mommy."

"Fetch Daddy the newspaper."

"It's not nice to bite your sister!"

"Daddy loves you, pookie ookums!"

Give me a break. I have yet to see any maternity wards for humans filled with puppies or kittens or baby gerbils.

Well, like I said, I was safe and sound, standing my ground firmly until a short time ago. Then I succumbed to family pressure. Before I could finish saying "Maybe . . ." we were homeward bound with a chocolate-colored standard poodle and about $500 worth of doggie toys, food, and a mansion-sized crate.

Nonetheless, I was bound and determined to remain strong. I knew that this critter would change our lives, but I would limit it to sensible changes. I would simply order the dog to do what I wanted. Not a problem.

Fortunately for all concerned, we happened to get the sweetest, most cooperative, and most intelligent puppy in the litter. Tallulah—we named her after the gorgeous actress Tallulah Bankhead—was the epitome of excellence.

She was so well potty trained that she would just bite my hand to let me know that she needed to go out. I adjusted well and found designer Band-Aids to match nearly every blouse I owned.

She was pro-Nancy too, totally into protecting my "image" around town. If I unwittingly put on a not-so-stunning outfit, Tallulah would just jump up on me, covering me with mud. I would run upstairs to change and suddenly realize how right she was. That color was just not me, the hem was a tad long, or I had made some other fashion faux pas.

One day I came home from work to find Tallulah had somehow reached our dinner napkin holder and shredded all the paper napkins. The kitchen floor was covered with them—under the table, under the dog crate, all around the stove and sink. I saw red, but as I knelt to start the tedious task at hand, I noticed the floor was filthy.

I suddenly realized what she was trying to tell me! Duh! Wash the kitchen floor. I gave her a big hug, and she confidently strutted over to her crate, knowing that I had finally gotten the message. And you think your dog's smart?

I still feel sorry for all those silly animal lovers and their nutty notions. What a relief that I am not subject to such foolish thinking about the status of mere animals. I am so thankful that God blessed me with an extraordinary pet.

This mommy is proud!

Small Wonder

Shane Galloway

Two years ago, still single and in my midthirties, I bought my first home—a stylish little 1938 ranch house that had certainly seen better days. Six and a half decades had inflicted miles of neglect and more than a few misguided remodeling efforts on the place. But amid the mess I saw good bones and plenty of art deco architectural charm. And in that curious state of magical thinking that visits the minds of many first-time home buyers, I convinced myself that I could whip the place into shape in a matter of months, throw a big, loud housewarming party, and move on to other matters in my life. Like finding a wife.

Instead, the projects began to line up in a seemingly endless succession of tasks, all vying for my attention, all costing time and money. My apartment-dwelling friends saw my venture as the happy acquisition of a piece of the American dream. But I quickly came to wonder if I'd just traded away some valuable peace of mind for a mere piece of property.

The work began with copious amounts of optimism and energy, as I spent long hours scraping ceilings, peeling wallpaper, and painting walls. But in my rush to make over the place into a decorator's dish, I ended up with a coarse mash of beiges that were too pink, whites that were too white, and a shocking red dining room that, while handsome on its own terms, looked like it was about ready to pull itself up from the foundations and move across town in a huff.

What the house really needed was an overhaul. In time the kitchen and bath would both require a good gutting; doors, moldings, and windows would need to be replaced, the aging wood floors refinished, the landscaping leveled and replanted. I began to secretly envy the young couples at church with their tidy, just-out-of-the-box tract homes, their his-and-hers to-do lists, their joint incomes and tax breaks—all the perks that can come with setting up house for two. It seemed nearly the whole of my prayer life in those days could be reduced to two simple words: *Help me.*

And then along came Sophie—unexpected, unbidden, and a little unkempt, looking for love at my back door. A small, delicate thing, looking like a slightly upsized, white Chihuahua, she took two small bounds up to my back patio late one evening and peered through the French doors as if to say, "Hello? Anyone home?" Equally startled and enchanted by this sight,

I opened my bedroom window and leaned down over the ledge to call to her. Without a moment's hesitation, she walked toward my open palms. I scooped her up like a fragile doll and took her inside.

Her teeth showed signs of age, but her eyes revealed an unblemished innocence—that remarkable quality Charles Dickens once attributed to children, as if they'd arrived on this earth "fresh from God." She was at home in my disheveled house, even if I wasn't, from the moment she arrived. That first night I let her into my bed, where she moved herself into the crook of my leg and fell fast asleep.

The rhythm of our friendship seemed familiar, as if she'd always been around somewhere on the edges of my life and decided it was time to take shape, walk up, and introduce herself. Each night after work, she'd dance around on her hind legs like a circus animal until I'd agree to pick her up and hold her. When I'd settle in to work at my desk, she would appear every few minutes at the door of my study to remind me of her presence, until finally I put a small hand towel on my desktop and laid her on it. There she'd curl up beneath my lamp, fix her gaze upon my face, and drift into slumber.

She was as gentle and unguarded a creature as I've ever seen. One night I went to visit a couple of friends and took her along for the trip. After a quick hug and chat at the door with my old chums, Sophie walked right up to their big, reclining Doberman and began curiously inspecting him. My friend's dog let out a long, low growl. But Sophie just continued her exploratory tour, and then, as if to make conversation with her new acquaintance, she stood alongside the dog's large head and peered unblinkingly into its eyes. When the dog refused to respond to her attentions, she moved right along to my friends' hairless cat, meeting the strange-looking creature head-on like a precocious child on the first day of school, eager to make new friends. She seemed to expect that every other creature in this world operated out of the same innate sense of goodwill that she did.

I attempted to find her owners and return her to her home, although it was immediately apparent that this dainty dog would be happy to devote her life to just about anyone, so long as they provided for her small needs—some attention at the end of the day, food, and a warm, small space in bed. Cradling her in my arms, I walked up and down the blocks around my house, looking for any sign of recognition from my neighbors.

There wasn't a trace. I took out an ad in the newspaper for two weeks without any response.

One afternoon I came across the most reasonable explanation I could find for her surprise appearance that late night. I'd taken Sophie with me to browse through antique shops on a Saturday. I felt awkward about it. I felt like I was beginning to resemble one of those women with a Yorkshire terrier stuffed into her handbag. But the day was too hot for me to leave her in my car alone, and I'd come to treasure her quiet company.

While I walked the shop floors, the older ladies made a fuss over her, petting her and exclaiming how sweet natured she was. When I explained how she had happened into my life, they shared a touching theory with me. They told me her master had possibly died. Oftentimes when a pet owner dies, his or her animal flees the vacant house. The ladies had seen it happen many times. The bond is broken, leaving the animal rootless, and it wanders off in search of a new purpose.

> Dogs love their friends and bite their enemies, quite unlike people, who are incapable of pure love and always have to mix love and hate.
>
> *Sigmund Freud*

I imagined that perhaps in grief or confusion, Sophie's instinct had pulled her in my direction while she searched for some semblance of the life she'd once had when her owner was alive.

Sophie stayed with me just three weeks. Nothing much

changed in the state of my house or in my position as a single man. But this dog, this vital little spark of an animal, visited me just long enough to gently nudge my attention away from my obsessions with paint chips and cracked plaster and marriage. She helped me close my fist around something dependable and turn my attentions back to the fixed point of what I know for sure in this life.

The present is unreliable; the future is a mystery. And a dog?

Well, a dog is the ebullient handiwork of the ever-creative mind of God. Dogs are free love in flesh and blood, right here in the day-to-day, offering themselves as gifts to us. They give up their affections and their devotion recklessly and serve to show us in a tangible way something that transcends what we know of other imperfect loves in this workaday world of demands and disappointments. Their message is simple. They are here to remind us, "You are loved."

I've come to see Sophie's brief visit in my life as a small wonder. Her unwavering gaze of devotion seemed miraculous at times, coming as it did so quickly from this enigmatic animal that stumbled into my life like a drunk from off the boulevard behind my house. She gave me reason to pause, to slow down, to relax, and to pay mind to the fullness of my life.

My busy life didn't allow for many more nights at home with Sophie, so I offered her to an acquaintance at my church. She was a woman who also lived alone and, I suspect, sometimes waded through her life with a measure of the same loneliness, the same challenges that I've experienced in mine as a "solo flyer."

And I imagined this dog, this startling animal, would do the same thing for her that she did for me. She would dance a tarantella on her hind legs each night when the woman returned home, and she would stare at her with her big gentle eyes, and she would burrow into the folds of her body at night in bed. And through these smallest of gestures, she would again and again serve to remind her of the loving and boundless heart of our God.

Kindred Spirits

Bernadine Johnson

Fiona was a good dog, a dog who had better character than most people. If you were in a hurry, she just got out of your way. She didn't have to be first. She always accepted an apology, no questions asked. When I was feeling sad, she just sat with me, not trying to reason anything out. She didn't ask for the best cut of meat or even for the largest portion but was extremely grateful for any small crumb that fell from the table. I was always greeted with what I called her "happy bark." She faithfully wagged her tail and made me feel important and loved every day, all the time.

I grew up watching the old *Lassie* series on television, envying first the young Tommy, then little Timmy (after Tommy evidently moved on to other television programs), for owning such a perfectly beautiful and smart dog. Fiona was our Lassie. She was a beautiful sable collie, a childhood fantasy fulfilled. Although she probably wouldn't have jumped into the water to save a life (she disliked her baths) or fought off dangerous and scary attackers as Lassie would have (she was scared of the vacuum cleaner), she never strayed from the yard and always let herself in and out of the door, both admirable qualities for a member of any family. Unlike my husband, Bob, she allowed me to dress her up in funny little hats for holidays and take her picture. Lassie allowed Timmy that kind of fun.

My three boys, all four years apart in age, grew up with Fiona. Her life with them is a visual delight, as each boy included her in their high school senior pictures. Our family room has "The Fiona Wall." She posed beautifully at ages two, six, and ten. The grayness of old age was clothing her sweet face in the last portrait, her final and most appropriately senior picture.

Jonathan, the youngest, was only six when baby Fiona came home with us. When she was two, Fiona raised her own little brood of baby Lassies. After they left the nest, Fiona started mothering Jonathan. Each night she climbed the stairs to the second floor bedrooms with him, jumped on the foot of his bed, and stayed there until he was asleep. She stayed with him through most of the night. She would then gently jump down and find her way to me, finishing the night on her own pillow next to my side of the bed. She always found her way to me. She was mine, and she knew it. We were the only females in the house, so we were bonded. We were both mothers. We both loved chocolate. Unbreakable bonds.

Fiona was an ordinary dog. But in our human lives where circumstances can change in the blink of an eye, where we sometimes have to hold on tightly as we feel our world spinning out of our control, we find great comfort in the ordinary. The passing of time is an ordinary event—unless, of course, it means watching someone or something you love grow old, arthritic, incontinent, and forgetful.

Watching her forget was the hardest part. My heart ached when she looked at me and would not wag her tail, when she didn't remember any of our memories, when she didn't get excited about M&M's anymore.

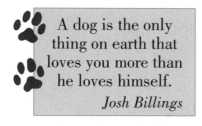

A dog is the only thing on earth that loves you more than he loves himself.
Josh Billings

That passing of time dropped in on us again and again. At first she needed help getting up on Jonathan's bed. Eventually she couldn't tackle the stairs. Jonathan, age eighteen, was sleeping alone.

In the spring of 2003, my husband came home with some exciting news (for him, not me). Apparently, over a year ago he had told someone at the local animal shelter to watch for a "nice collie," and now they had one. I was the most surprised by the fact that we had never talked this idea over together. Married people are supposed to do that. My conscience quickly reminded me that I've bought a lot of things I've never talked over with him first, so I let him off the hook.

However, I still had no interest in the collie. By this time I was carrying Fiona up and down stairs to ease the discomfort in her legs. I couldn't imagine having a good attitude while taking care of a big old dog and a big new dog. I also still vividly remembered having two dogs for a time during my childhood and not knowing which one to love the most. Nobody had told me that it was okay to love both of them at the same time. I had spent a lot of time sitting near the doghouse, confused and crying. I wondered, forty years later, if I still had that personality disorder. I rationalized that I had done okay with having three boys, so maybe I shouldn't panic. After checking out the collie himself, Bob urged me to go and just look at her. He thought I would be surprised.

It was a nice surprise. I encountered a young Fiona look-alike. She was beautiful, sweet, and happy to see me. Still uncertain, I went back with Bob the next day and took her for a walk. Bob was convinced that we needed to bring her home. I agreed to put my child-hood fears behind me and follow his intuition. We named her Maggie. She seemed to like the name. She wagged her tail and smiled her collie smile.

Maggie attached herself to me like a mosquito that had found a great blood supply. She quickly became my shadow. She brought activity and laughter and barking back into the house immediately, prancing around with Fiona's old toys in her mouth, urging us to play. Maggie Mae (the middle name added by Son #2) quickly learned to recognize the sound of the M&M jar, thus provoking her little dance which said, "I know chocolate isn't good for dogs, but one little M&M won't kill a big dog like me!" We began to fall in love with each other. She was afraid of the staircase to the second floor, which was okay with me. I figured it would be less collie hair to vacuum, and Jonathan was used to sleeping alone by now.

I'll never know for sure what was going on in the mind of my precious Fiona, but I think she somehow knew she could leave us now. Bob and I were gone that Sunday, two weeks after Maggie's adoption, when Fiona had a stroke. Jonathan, who was home from college, held her in his arms, put his ear to her nose, and heard her last breath. It was a hard thing for a boy. He had to do a man's job and be strong of heart.

We gave her a big send-off and buried her. Robert Louis Stevenson once said, "You do not think dogs will be in heaven? I tell you, they will be there before any of us." Because of Fiona, I have a tendency to believe Mr. Stevenson. And I hope she gets all the M&M's she wants, since they won't be able to hurt her there.

I once read in a magazine a touching epitaph to a coon dog named Track: "He wasn't the best, but he was the best I ever had." Fiona was an ordinary dog, the best we ever had, who made our lives anything but ordinary. Is faithfulness ordinary? Is forgiveness ordinary? Is love?

That night Jonathan asked if Maggie could come upstairs and sleep on his bed. I was quick to agree, but he'd have to find a way to get the eighty-five-pound puppy up the stairs. After being carried up part of the way and then lured with a hot dog, she found her way to Jonathan's bed and immediately jumped up, cuddling up to him. On a night when there could have been much sadness in the house, I heard laughter. Jonathan, who was forced to start the day as a man, ended the day as Timmy, the boy, with his Lassie beside him, loving him up. Maggie gave him that gift. And when he was asleep, she gently jumped down and found her way to me. Kindred spirits need to be close.

I've started calling her my angel dog because she seems to have come to us as a gift from heaven. One goes up. One comes down. I know she was sent to us at the perfect time. Now if I could just keep her off of the couches. She thinks they're her own personal clouds to plop on.

And Gracie
Makes Three

Michael K. Walker

When I was growing up, our home was a menagerie with six children and a host of other non-human animals. Always dogs and cats, at times aquariums full of fish, the occasional bird—remember, we had cats—and once even a monkey. Naturally, pets were a fact of life, like God or air.

Lucky was our dog with nine lives, who lived up to her name by surviving several near-death experiences. In those pre–leash law days, she used to wander the neighborhood. My older brother saw her one morning, blocks away from home, behind the Sambo's restaurant. Lucky had made friends with the cook, who would toss scraps out the back door. This, we learned, was a regular occurrence. Our dog actually went out for breakfast.

Pet Insurance

It's not as new as you might think. Veterinary Pet Insurance, the oldest and largest health insurance company for pets in the United States, wrote its first policy for one of the nine dogs who played Lassie. As of this writing, the company covers over 400,000 policies. Currently more dogs are insured than cats, and both numbers go up every year. Recently the American Society for the Prevention of Cruelty to Animals began offering its own health insurance, and health coverage for animals is an employee perk in some corporations.[3]

Shepherd-mix Hannibal was my companion from kindergarten through my sophomore year in college. Mom brought home three pups from the same litter, and of course they loved to roughhouse. So we named them Caesar, Brutus (as in *Et tu, Brute?*), and Hannibal—the general who led the elephants over the Alps to attack Rome. Later, we even had a Labrador named Hercules. Is it any wonder I studied Latin in high school?

My sisters always had cats, so we often had kittens. In fact, one year Karina and her grown-up daughter Tanya both had babies in the same month. I'm not sure if anyone, including the cats, knew which kittens went with which litter. Both mamas nursed any kitten that was hungry. All in the family, I guess.

"Stray" was the cat who found us. She showed up one evening, looking like she'd been hit by a car. Her forehead was scabbed over and tail broken; her stomach was bloated from near starvation. We fed her several times, though we could not catch her to take her to the vet. She decided to stay but wouldn't come inside or let us touch her. It was months before anyone could hold her. It seemed natural to name her Stray.

Later we discovered the reason for her mistrust. She had too many healed wounds for them to be accidental. And the scar on her throat explained why she could not meow like other cats. Yet in spite of her past, she became beautiful and sleek, with a certain air of nobility.

Once while watching a TV show about a company that sold royal crests for pets, we decided that Stray deserved a crest. Suddenly we realized her name was totally inadequate for her personality and countenance. That was the evening she was dubbed Stray Elizabeth Victoria Catherine Crestworthy IX (she was our ninth cat).

Though the rest of the family called her Stray Elizabeth, I in my teenaged guy humor usually pronounced it Stray Lizard Breath.

After I moved away from home, my lifestyle and work

> If you pick up a starving dog and make him prosperous, he will not bite you; that is the principal difference between a dog and a man.
>
> *Mark Twain*

schedules did not allow for pets. Even after meeting, falling in love with, and marrying my wife Laura, life was too "on the go" to consider letting an animal into our lives.

Then, the day after our first wedding anniversary, Laura was diagnosed with cancer. Though it was caught early and Laura recovered, children would not be an option for us. As we came to peace with this, we realized our lives could be full with just the two of us.

We bought a house and were busy with church and careers, but I think in a way we were unsettled. Though she had not grown up with pets, Laura knew how much I wanted a dog, so she was open to the idea, provided the dog met her criteria: it would have to be cocker spaniel–sized, have short hair, and be caramel colored, and there could be no big wagging tail to knock the pretty teacups off the decorative tables.

This agreed upon, the timing never seemed right, so we did not pursue the matter.

Then one Saturday morning we woke up with nothing on the agenda for the day. Out of the blue one of us mentioned perhaps going to look at dogs. So off we went to the SPCA. No luck. Only big dogs, so we left. But at least we'd made a big step toward actually adopting a pet.

On the way home I suggested we swing by the pound. Again no luck, but just as we were about to leave, I casually struck up a conversation with another customer. Slowly I became aware that we were being interviewed.

The lady worked with a rescue organization and thought we might be a good match for a little white spitz that needed a home. Would we be interested in following her and meeting the dog? We said sure, why not?

Our lives have never been the same.

Scrawny and rather odd looking—she looked more like a white fox than a dog—she was the right size, she had mostly short hair, and her tail curled up over her back. Wagging would not be a problem. But she was white, not caramel colored. Laura was dubious. Since the dog was obviously a sweetheart, we agreed to take her home for a trial run.

On the drive home, as the frightened little creature shivered in her arms, Laura named her Grace, after Grace Kelly. Shortly thereafter, Gracie threw up on Laura's foot. At that moment Laura became a mommy. And Gracie became a princess.

It turned out that she was underweight and had a bad case of worms. That explained the strange fox-like appearance. Once healthy, that short-haired dog with a cute, curly tail was transformed into a gorgeous American Eskimo. With *very* long hair.

But the greater transformation was within Laura. Gracie became the child we thought we would never have. We didn't care that white hair constantly covered our dark carpeting. Or about the muddy paw prints. Or about the squeaky toys littering the living room.

Never before had Laura known the unconditional love that only a dog can give.

Though my sophisticated wife swore she would never talk baby talk to a dog, with Gracie she lasted only one day. And though Laura swore the dog would never be allowed on the bed, this lasted less than a week.

The rest of the furniture? Gracie's. Her favorite spot is on the arm of the overstuffed chair where she can see out the front window. And the couch is hers as well—she sits not just on the seat cushions but also atop the back, like Snoopy on his doghouse.

Have you ever noticed how parents seem to add the child's middle name during a scolding? Laura soon added the middle name to "Grace Elizabeth." She did it, not I.

Though Gracie was a smart dog, no one had ever spent time training her. She learned "sit" in just a couple minutes, along with several other tricks. I even got her to play the piano. Standing on her hind feet, her nose even with the keys, we play a mean "Heart and Soul" duet, though her favorite song is "Für Elise."

I've heard it said that dogs are like perpetual toddlers. They have limited communication ability, but they're always happy to be with you. Even better, canines never become teenagers. Plus you don't have to worry about college tuition or orthodontia.

Our canine daughter has been with us for seven years now. Whenever Mommy comes home, Gracie stands on her hind feet and waves her paws in the air (her way of saying "please") until Mommy picks her up for a hug. Strangely, when Daddy comes home, she often grabs a toy and runs into the other room squeaking it until I come to greet her there. Go figure.

Truly, Gracie was a gift from God to help both Laura and me feel settled. We're a family of three now, and life has its daily routines. Gracie would not have it otherwise. One of our routines is exercise.

We've met many of our neighbors while walking the dog. Our four-footed companion opens the door for many conversations. Though I may not remember the names of all the humans on our block, I know the names of most of the dogs. And everyone knows Gracie.

Once I was way across town and was startled by a complete stranger who blurted, "I know you. You live in my neighborhood. You have that white dog."

Of all the animals we had while I was growing up, I've never known a pet more perfectly suited than our Gracie is to us. The timing that put us at the pound at the very moment the rescue lady was there is proof enough to me that miracles happen.

Isn't that just like God? Knowing what we need even before we do. Prompting us, out of the blue, to say, "Let's go look for a dog."

A Real-Life Lassie

Virginia Bowen

His name was Cap'n Beau. I have no idea how he got his name; I don't even recall his owners. I do know he was my neighbor—and my guardian angel.

It was the early 1960s. The original *Lassie* TV series had just gone off the air after an eight-year run. Everyone knew the "Lassie" look of the rough collie and knew that any "Lassie" was a friend and protector to children everywhere. In my world, I knew they were right. Cap'n Beau was a rough collie, mahogany sable, just like the male dogs that played Lassie on TV.

I was three or four years old and a very shy new kid on the block, recently transported from Texas to a smallish city in Florida no one had heard of at the time—Orlando. My parents tried to get me some friends. I have vague memories of some little girls who lived nearby coming to play. I do recall that with five older brothers and sisters and their friends coming and going, what I really wanted was to be left alone. Alone with my true friends—the neighborhood pets. While I only vaguely recall the masses of people that came through our house in the year or so we lived next door to Cap'n Beau, I vividly recall him.

This propensity to befriend animals was not a new thing for me, even at that tender age. It has stayed with me my whole life. Like a little Doctor Doolittle, I had a knack for talking with the animals. In this same neighborhood there was a cat, calico I believe, that came to our back porch every day to visit. My sister swears to this day that when I was not at home, she could go to the door and tell the cat, "Virginia's not here right now," and off the cat would go, completing her rounds of the neighborhood, returning later for our visit.

Cap'n Beau, however, was special among the animals in the neighborhood. We shared a property line. This was back before "good fences make good neighbors," back when neighbors actually knew each other's names and people cared about what their neighbors thought of them—and cared about each other. Dogs were not left to roam but somehow knew their boundaries and held to them. Our "fence" was a line of hedges. Being in subtropical Florida, they were healthy, thick

> Anybody who doesn't know what soap tastes like never washed a dog.
> Franklin P. Jones

shrubs, probably azaleas. Everyone in Orlando had azaleas back then.

Cap'n Beau never, ever left his side of those bushes. But there were bare spots between the branches and where leaves had been eaten out by insects. Cap'n Beau and I would visit there, in those bare spots. I would lie on the grass on one side, he on the other, and we would talk in the way that only children and dogs can talk to each other. I would reach through and pet his wonderfully thick, soft fur and probably fed him treats on occasion.

Looking into his soft, brown eyes that appeared to be all-wise, I told him my dreams. I confided secrets I told no other living being. My mother got to know his owners so that I could go next door and see him in his own yard as a special treat from time to time. Mostly, though, we visited through those bushes—the imaginary fence that Cap'n Beau never crossed.

It's funny the things we remember about our childhood when we're all grown up and life has blown us here and there with our worries and mortgages and car payments and jobs. I remember Cap'n Beau and the day he saved me. It was nothing as dramatic as pulling Timmy from a well or running for help because some enormous tree had fallen on me. It was just him coming to the side of a frightened little girl, his friend, in her own backyard.

A strange dog had come into the yard while I was playing that day. Being the little Doctor Doolittle I was, I went over to say hello. But this dog was not friendly. He was hostile. Perhaps he was hungry, lost, and frightened. Maybe he was in pain. I'll never know, because the moment he growled at me, causing me to cry out, Cap'n Beau broke through his "fence." He tore down a bush as he crashed over to my aid. Teeth bared and snarling, he chased the strange dog away, down the street, then quickly returned to my side in our yard, where he sat with me while I cried. I hugged his neck and felt his comfort. After a moment, when I was less afraid, he barked, then barked again, until my mother came out to see what was wrong. When I was safely in her arms, he went back into his yard and never again crossed that line of bushes.

We moved away just a few months later. I never saw Cap'n Beau after that, and now he is long, long gone. That was forty years ago. But he will never be gone in my heart, even after all this time. I've never tried to replace him in my life with another collie, because I know he never can be replaced. He taught me that while all animals may not be my friends, the friendly ones are true. There's a special spot in me just for him. When I see a brave, proud silhouette of a collie on a hill, I don't think Lassie, I think Cap'n Beau. My friend and my angel.

A Very Large Gift

Joan Guest

Nori was fifteen years old and missing her sister, who'd gone off to college. She'd asked for a dog loads of times, but I'd never taken her request very seriously. We had a cat, and my ninety-six-year-old mother-in-law lived with us, so my typically flippant response to Nori was, "We'll get a dog when the cat or Grandma leaves."

This time, though, Nori surprised me. "Mom, I've saved eighty dollars from doing chores. That should be enough to pay for a dog and the vet bills for his first shots." She went on to recite all the usual things a kid says to convince a parent that she will spend infinite amounts of time caring for an animal. *Well,* I thought as we passed the pound on the way home from her cello lesson, *maybe we should look and see what we find.*

We stopped by the pound, and there in the parking lot a family "pushing" their dog accosted my daughter. "Are you adopting a dog? We'd like our dog to go to a family with kids. Please adopt him." He was a little Pomeranian, and by the sound of it he was well trained and friendly. We needed a dog that would not require training, as we didn't have the time for that. We also needed a dog that might like to sit on my mother-in-law's lap. I wondered if maybe Providence was taking a hand here and managing our choice.

When Grandma had come to us, she was expected to live only a year or two. Seven years later, she was very frail, blind, hard of hearing, and confused but still social. She wanted people to sit with her all evening while she watched TV. We couldn't do that unless we had a chore we could do in the den. We had thought the orphaned kitten we adopted would be an answer, but like many cats, he wanted almost nothing to do with people.

So Grandma wandered in the evenings, looking for someone to be with her. She'd call down to me or my husband where we were inevitably working on our computers on a lower level. Because she was hard of hearing, we could not call back to her. We'd have to stop what we were doing and go to her to tell her loudly where we were and what we were doing. Fifteen minutes later she'd be back again, calling for someone. When the kids were younger, they'd watched TV with her in the evenings. But high school schedules and Grandma's tendency to talk over all the TV shows

Do You Hear Bells?

American poet Robert Frost and his dog, Gillie, lived in the backwoods of Vermont. From the valley below, Frost's secretary could communicate with him by means of a line attached to a bell. When Frost grew too old to hear the bell, Gillie would hear it and fetch his master.[4]

meant that she was now rarely joined by the kids. And then there was only one kid left at home.

So we put in our request for this middle-aged Pomeranian. For a week Nori waited while the pound checked out the dog to see if it could be adopted. For seven days she prayed the dog would be hers. For seven days my husband and I prayed that if it was not wise for us to have this animal, God would prevent it. We were not convinced at all that taking on the care of a dog—even a middle-aged one—was a wise idea. My two jobs, my husband's home-based business, our two kids, our two elderly mothers—weren't those enough to take up our time? Should the adolescent needs of a fifteen-year-old really take precedence in a household so overburdened already? I felt strongly that a kitten would be a much better choice for our daughter.

Seven days later, we got the word: no. The pound said the dog had become aggressive after leaving his family and had to be given to a Pomeranian rescue group that could deal with the behavior. The pound would not allow him to be adopted. Nori was crushed. As a family we made an appointment to go back to the pound to pick out a kitten. I'd seen several litters there when we had last visited. I was sure we'd find a good kitten.

When we got to the pound, our daughter asked to take one last look at the dogs. Since she had made a wise choice before (passing over the large puppies and yappy tiny breeds), I said yes. As it turned out, all the dogs had signs on them such as, "Aggressive female. Should go only to family experienced with dog handling." Only one pen did not have such a sign. There sat "Samson," a gigantic six-year-old black German shepherd. As Samson wagged his tail, the staff member sang his praises. He never barked, was exceptionally well trained, and was very gentle. Nori asked to take him out of his cage, and he trotted around with her, sat on command, came when called, and never jumped in her face. The staff member told us why he had been put up for adoption and then said, "I doubt you'd care about this, but Samson is so gentle that we've been taking him to the nursing home next door to do pet therapy with the elderly." That clinched it. Within thirty minutes, Samson was hopping (make that tripping—he's rather clumsy) into our car for the ride home.

Now Samson's been with us almost two months. Nori has her dog and her friend for life. She has someone to listen to her when Mom or Dad is mad at her.

But even more remarkable is that Grandma has company. Grandma doesn't wander anymore. Instead, Samson sits at her feet, and she pats his head all evening long. Since he's large and black, her legally blind eyes can usually make him out against the light-colored rug. He sleeps next to her bed at night and puts his head under the covers when it thunders. They are each other's new best friends.

Caregiving? Yes, we've got a lot of it going on at our house. Getting a dog was not a self-evidently wise decision. But God knew what we didn't—that we needed a dog more than we knew.

Ace, a Companion Extraordinaire

Robert Lloyd Russell

My dad was killed in an industrial accident when I was one, leaving my mom to cope with three children under the age of six. My sister was older than I and my brother was the oldest. This was during the 1940s, and our summers were spent with my Uncle Chuck and Aunt Ann on one of the sparsely populated Gulf Islands on Canada's west coast. Uncle Chuck had been a Royal Canadian Air Force fighter pilot and a true WWII "ace" who, in the course of many dogfights, shot down numerous enemy airplanes and was himself shot down three times behind enemy lines. More important, he was my only father figure as a young child. Aunt Ann was a very proper Londoner who adjusted well to remote living with an open well, an outhouse, and little in the way of earthly possessions. They lived alone, and my siblings and I were "their kids" during each summer.

Chuck and Ann's only pet was a wonderful Chesapeake Bay retriever named Ace. Family legend is that he was the only straight-haired puppy in the litter but as he grew became the only curly-haired adult from the litter.

I could tell many remarkable stories about Ace. He was often sent to the only store on the island, a distance of nearly six miles each way, with a note on his collar. The store owner could send raw red meat wrapped in butcher paper on the return trip, and Ace would dutifully deliver it to us without so much as puncturing the paper on the trip home. Ace was obedient to his master and seemed to have an unquestioning loyalty and love for his master—and his master's family.

During those summers there once was a forest fire on a neighboring island. Like most able-bodied island men, Uncle Chuck responded, and after many hours of intense work near the hot end of a bucket brigade, he needed to catch some rest and fell asleep propped against the trunk of a majestic Douglas fir tree. The fire continued to spread. Sensing danger, Ace began furiously licking Chuck, to no avail. Suddenly Ace took Chuck's shirt sleeve and tugged enough to pull him away from the trunk of the tree— enough so that my uncle awoke and scrambled away with Ace just as a burning branch fell where he had been sleeping. Many other stories of Ace doing the

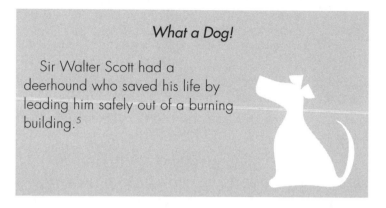

What a Dog!

Sir Walter Scott had a deerhound who saved his life by leading him safely out of a burning building.[5]

right thing in the right way have endeared Ace to our family members.

The story closest to my heart occurred when I was about six and my brother ten. The two of us were out fishing for salmon in the nearby straits. Ace accompanied us; he loved to go where we went, especially when it was in a boat. We often went out in a small wooden rowboat with a small outboard motor since the bays and open water were quite sheltered—we only had to watch for the wake of larger vessels and for approaching storms. Porpoises would often play alongside our craft.

The day was especially majestic with beautiful weather, calm water, great fishing, and Ace by our side. Now, many years later, neither my brother nor I remember exactly what caused me to stand up in the boat. Suddenly, without warning, I was in the water as the boat continued on. Not being an accomplished swimmer, coupled with being surprised and frightened, I began to flail around in the water. My brother began to turn the boat slowly, so as not to create bigger waves—but it was taking too long.

By the time my brother had begun turning the boat, Ace was in the water swimming toward me. He reached me long before the boat did. The first thing Ace did was grab in his jaws a wad of my shirt, high on one of my shoulders. Never once did he let go. Ace provided a sense of calm as his powerful body stayed tightly against me. My brother was able to bring the boat gently to me. If Ace had not been the faithful companion that he was, my guardian angel on that day, I am sure I would not be here to testify or write this eulogy to a most wonderful dog who fulfilled his mission on earth and departed many years ago.

Recently my wife of thirty-five years and I visited the island, and many memories flooded upon me. Some things have changed; for example, my aunt and uncle now share a headstone on the island, and their homestead is now part of a new national park. But my childhood memories and love for Ace have endured.

TOP 10 DOG MOVIES OF ALL TIME

I fell in dog love a little later in life than most—thirty-nine, thanks to an adorable little American Eskimo named Gracie—but I've always been a sucker for dogs on the silver screen. I mean, c'mon, who doesn't love Lassie? Or those too-cute 101 Dalmatians? "Get down, Lucky!" Or the courageous Buck in *The Call of the Wild*?

I've also shed buckets of tears over my fair share of tug-at-the-heartstrings doggy tearjerkers. (You'd have to have a heart of stone not to cry at *Old Yeller.*) So in honor of those beloved canines who have filled the silver screen and our hearts, I've come up with a list of favorite dog movies. (Narrowing it down to a mere ten was impossible, so I've included some honorable mentions at the end.) My picks, in no particular order:

1. **Old Yeller**—The 1957 Disney drama of the yellow mongrel stray and the boy who reluctantly adopted him, then grew to love him. Try to make it through without crying. Just try.

2. **Lady and the Tramp**—A sheer delight that stands the test of time. And definitely the most romantic dog movie around. Nothing beats Tramp and Lady in that spaghetti-eating scene. And of course you can't beat the indomitable Peggy Lee singing "He's a Tramp."

3. **Lassie Come Home** (the first of the Lassie flicks)—The classic about the faithful collie who travels a thousand miles from northern Scotland to England to return to the boy she loves (Roddy McDowall). It was one of the biggest-grossing films of 1943, and it has touched generations of dog-loving audiences ever since. Lassie climbs mountains, swims rivers, fights other dogs, and does whatever it takes to get home to her beloved master. Eye candy includes the picturesque pastoral countryside and a young Elizabeth Taylor.

4. **My Dog Skip**—A 2000 film based on the bestselling memoir by the late Willie Morris and starring Frankie Muniz from *Malcolm in the Middle* TV fame, this ranks up there with *Lassie Come Home* about the love of a boy and his dog—except this one's a Jack Russell terrier. Fabulous!

5. **Lad, a Dog**—Angela Cartwright plays a handicapped little girl who finds love, understanding, and healing in a beloved collie in this 1962 film that also starred Peter Breck—one of the gorgeous Barkley brothers from the sixties TV show *The Big Valley*. From the Victorian classic novel by Albert Payson Terhune. (But be forewarned: you'll need an entire box of tissues for the ending.)

6. **101 Dalmatians**—The Disney animated classic with all those darling spotted puppies makes me warm and mushy every time I see it. The real-live-people remake with Glenn Close as the evil Cruella DeVil is fun, but nothing beats the original!

7. Greyfriars Bobby—A lesser-known 1961 Disney drama starring Donald Crisp (the father from *National Velvet*), based on the true story of the devoted Scottish dog who refused to be separated from his master—even in death. This wee Skye terrier slept every night on his owner's grave in the cemetery of Greyfriars Church for fourteen years. Bobby is now buried with his beloved master, and today there's a statue to him on a street corner in Edinburgh. Talk about man's best friend.

8. Homeward Bound: The Incredible Journey—The 1993 remake of the original Disney classic with the voice talents of Don Ameche, Michael J. Fox, and Sally Field as the three animals who overcome amazing obstacles to find their way home. Inspiring.

9. Beethoven—In a word? Hilarious! How can it not be when you mix Charles Grodin and a St. Bernard? Anytime you need a good laugh, rent this.

10. Shiloh—Who wouldn't love the story of Shiloh, a beagle who escapes his abusive owner, finds a young boy, and follows him home? Will Marty get to keep Shiloh? Watch and see in this 1996 film based on the Newbery Award–winning book by Phyllis Reynolds Naylor.

Honorable Mentions: *A Dog of Flanders, Because of Winn-Dixie, The Shaggy Dog, Benji*, Toto in *The Wizard of Oz*, Asta in *The Thin Man* series, *All Dogs Go to Heaven, Far from Home: The Adventures of Yellow Dog, Turner and Hooch*, and last but definitely not least, Rin Tin Tin "The Wonder Dog." This German shepherd was one of Hollywood's top stars in the 1920s and early '30s. He captivated audiences with his amazing stunts and rescues, and at the height of his career, he received 10,000 letters a week. He also had his own production unit, limo, and chauffeur, and his descendants starred in the TV series *The Adventures of Rin Tin Tin*, which ran in reruns until 1964.

Becoming Alpha
Callie Smith Grant

She came to me when I was in no shape to have pets. I was trying to get through a full term of community college without dropping out so I could transfer to a university, but I was having trouble with focus. I had dropped out of college three times already. I had made friends with people who were going nowhere fast, and I had a boyfriend with whom I could see I would have no future.

As if all that weren't enough, while I was at work one night, my two roommates moved out of our rented house without telling me, taking with them my just-paid rent and even my damage deposit. Now I would have to move too. I was working midnights as a waitress, going to classes in the mornings, and trying to sleep during the day. None of this was doing much for my self-esteem.

But sometimes a dog chooses us. Or maybe that dog is sent to us. At any rate, I met this one at the house of some relatives several blocks from the house I was going to have to leave. She was a mixed breed, maybe German shepherd and sheltie, according to a veterinarian later on. She was a medium-sized dog with a thick golden coat, rather longish hair, and a plumed tail. She was one of those dogs who look like they have on black eyeliner and black lipstick, and she "smiled."

She had parked herself under a stoop at my relatives' place and given birth to eight puppies, clearly her first litter. My relatives found her, hungry and bewildered, and they fed her. Though I was not the one who fed her, for some reason when I peeked under the stoop at the new nursing puppies, that dog's eyes locked on me like she'd been waiting her whole life for me. She thumped her tail on the ground a few times, stood up, and dropped all those nursing babies one by one as she hurried to me. I laughed and coaxed her back to her puppies. She might have been a lousy mother, but she hooked me immediately.

I helped find homes for all the puppies. I even found a home for the mother, but she turned out to be too high-strung to be around the children of the house, and she was returned to my relatives. I would eventually learn that this dog was afraid of children, cats, trucks, men in uniforms, anyone with a deep and loud voice, and brooms. Clearly her earlier days had been rough ones.

She visited my house once, riding over in a car with my relatives, and then the next day I found her at my back door, wanting to come inside. She had figured out where she wanted to be and how to get there. So what was I to do? I scrounged up money for shots and spaying, and I kept her. At this time I was stumbling my way through German class, so I named her Freunde, the German word for female friend, and began speaking to her in very primitive German. I had a bilingual dog, more or less.

Eventually, as expected, I had to leave the house where I was living, so that autumn Freunde and I moved to the country. That's one way to put it. The other way is to say that we moved to a one-room trailer on a dirt road a long way from town. The trailer was so ancient and so settled that calling it a mobile home would simply be a mistake, although it actually had a fin on top of it, like a 1957 Chevy. Under the fin inside the trailer was a tiny loft with room for a double mattress. I was too claustrophobic for that; I slept in a bed downstairs.

I was responsible for filling my own propane tank, and I was not able to afford that until Thanksgiving. This was chilly Great Lakes country, so Freunde slept in the bed with me under a sleeping bag. We kept one another warm. And we bonded.

I have fond and not-so-fond memories of that time. The fond memories are of walking the countryside with Freunde in all that autumn glory, watching her romp through a pumpkin patch or nose through a pile of leaves, feeding her steak scraps from work, taking her everywhere with me in my car. I was amazed at this personal experience with a dog. We always had dogs when I was growing up, but they were family pets. I had never before been an alpha to a dog. It was a beautiful and humbling experience. Freunde was responsive to my tone and mood, and it was flattering how eager she was to be with me. In her own way, she kept me from isolating myself too much.

I *was* isolating. It was easy to do as a third-shift worker, and at this time in my life I was also broke and depressed and too proud to ask anyone for help on either count. I simply kept Freunde with me as much as possible. I felt secure with her. I felt like I knew what I was doing with her. She seemed to think I was amazing, even though I felt like a complete loser. I kept on stumbling along.

One night, however, I had a mini dark night of the soul. It was as if God wrote out the story of my adult life so far and scrolled it right in front of me. It revealed so much. I fully realized all of a sudden that I was messing up my own life, and nobody was doing it for me. The school president and honor student who had been voted Most Likely to Succeed was doing everything possible not to succeed. In fact, I was hurting myself.

That night I sank to my knees in that dinky trailer and cried all night long. Freunde was there with me the whole time. She whined and nosed my ribs and licked my face, those sweet brown eyes showing such concern. I cried into her fur, and she let me. I cried until I could cry no more. Then I prayed. Eventually I fell asleep curled around Freunde, and when I woke up in the morning, I felt peace for the first time in years.

That day I had a long talk with my folks, who were thrilled that I intended to stop what they rather generously called spinning my wheels. Over the next few weeks, I gently let go of many of my so-called friends. I broke up with my boyfriend, much to my dog's delight—she'd never liked him. I got a roommate so I could stop isolating myself (she slept in that awful loft in the fin). The roommate brought with her a dog companion for Freunde named Cowboy. Soon I was accepted at a university in the next county.

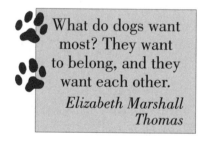

What do dogs want most? They want to belong, and they want each other.
Elizabeth Marshall Thomas

I knew I could not take Freunde with me. It broke my heart, but I had to face it. Fortunately the people who lived next door to me on the dirt road were happy to take her in. She became their family dog and lived a good long life with them. I'm not sure if Freunde's presence was as powerful in their home as in mine. Truly that dog helped me cope, and in the process, she gave me some pleasure and even a little confidence.

I got through college and have gone on to live a good, productive life. I did not have another pet for the next twenty years. Now I'm in a place in my life where I have pets, and once again, they found me. Their presence in my home is as powerful and as God-sent as my Freunde's presence was back when I was, as my folks gently put it, spinning my wheels.

The Four-Legged Daughter

Candace Carteen

My husband and I got married later in life, so we together decided that children were not in our future. But after about a year, we started feeling like something was missing in our relationship. Within two years we decided that a child would be a very happy addition to our lives, and we started working on getting pregnant.

Several months passed; nothing was happening. One night after a long, tearful, and heated conversation, we decided that we would start with a dog. And work our way up to a baby. We had no idea what that decision would bring us.

We found out about a puppy from a friend who suggested a breeder. We contacted her. "No," she said, "I'm not planning on breeding any more. But I do have a little girl puppy that my sister was going to take and she decided not to. Would you like to see her?"

We said "Sure," and headed out to the middle of nowhere to see this little schnauzer puppy. As we drove through the countryside, we discussed our impending "purchase."

"She said the puppy was three hundred dollars. Let's offer her two hundred and see if she'll take it." We both agreed.

As we drove up the long gravel driveway to this woman's home, we saw a baby playpen in the front yard. As we pulled up to the pen, we noticed a little ball of black and gray fur stand up on its hind legs and bark at us. Our eyes never left the smiling pup as we exited the car and surrounded the playpen.

By the time the owner joined us, we had already removed the puppy from its cage and begun trading kisses. We also knew that any price she asked for the puppy would be paid. She was ours!

About six months after Harmony came into our lives, the infertility treatments started. As we began to realize that pregnancy was not going to come easily, we also realized that this little puppy had captured our hearts.

Like a baby, she needed almost constant care. During the days when both George and I worked, Harmony was taken to my mother's for "child care." There Harmony had my mother and her poodle Anne to play with. During the evenings and weekends, Harmony loved to watch movies and go fishing with us. She appeared to be happy no matter where she was, as long as "Mom and Dad" were there.

One night not long after we celebrated her second birthday, Harmony woke me up whining. I reached down to the bottom of the bed where she always slept and found her sitting in a pool of fluid. I quickly picked her up and headed toward the kitchen.

George woke up, concerned, and called to me down the hall. "What's wrong?"

As I sat Harmony on the floor, I watched as her little feet simply slid out from underneath her. I grabbed a kitchen towel and placed her wet body down on it. When I called to her, all she could do was whine. She then tried with all her power to come to me. I watched as her little head wobbled back and forth and then fell to the floor.

"I don't know," I screamed, wiping the tears from my eyes with the back of my hand. "But we need to rush her to emergency."

That's all George had to hear. He was out of bed, dressed, and heading to the car almost before I had a chance to wrap Harmony in a soft, pink blanket and throw a robe on.

We called the veterinary hospital as we drove, and they were ready for us when we arrived. They took her limp body from my arms and headed toward a back room. We sat there for what seemed like hours before one of the doctors called us into a private room.

"You have one sick little girl. It appears that she has diabetes."

Eyes Wide Shut

Sir Winston Churchill adored his poodle Rufus. One night while watching the film *Oliver Twist* with some friends, Churchill held Rufus on his lap. During the scene where Bill Sikes is about to drown his dog, Churchill covered Rufus's eyes and said, "Don't look now, dear. I'll tell you about it afterwards."[6]

"What?" we both said at once.

"How could that be?" I asked. "She's had checkups every six months since we got her."

"I guess no one caught the signs. Has she been drinking a lot lately?"

"She's always drunk a lot. She's an active little girl."

"Well, we'll need to keep her overnight for testing and observation." The doctor then made a big mistake as he said, "You can call anytime to see how she's doing."

I was on the phone every hour on the hour. "How is she? Is she any better? Is she sleeping? Do you know any more?"

By the next afternoon I had made twelve calls. I think they were tired of hearing from me, but no one complained.

Harmony spent the next five days in the hospital. Before we were allowed to take her home, we were instructed on how to give shots and monitor her glucose.

I didn't think I could do that. I was afraid of needles. Now I was being told that I would have to give our four-legged daughter shots twice a day. No, no, no, no, no! Not me! George would have to it.

By the first morning, I knew that the role of shot-giver would be all mine due to our work schedules. As I filled the syringe to the proper level, I knew I had to reach beyond my own feelings and fears and protect my baby from the ravages of diabetes. So I did the deed. Harmony gave me a big, wet kiss.

As time went on, I got really good at giving shots, and Harmony came to me to receive them. We both grew to understand that it was necessary.

Then one day it became my turn to receive shots. All that we had done so far regarding our infertility had failed. Now it was time to go for in vitro fertilization. That meant that George would now be giving *me* shots twice a day. The first night, Harmony followed us into the bathroom and sat positioned right by the sink so that I couldn't miss seeing her. As George injected the first needle, Harmony licked my leg and then laid her head on my foot. I cried—not from the shot but because of her concern. For weeks the ritual continued, and Harmony was always there.

Finally my ordeal stopped. The treatments weren't working. I was not getting pregnant. Over the months we also discovered that Harmony's treatment was not as successful as we had hoped. Her diabetes was extremely hard to control. Even with testing, we couldn't keep her glucose levels steady. She was back in the hospital for a week.

We were now required to "dip" her urine twice a day as well as test her blood. The three of us got into the new routine, and it became second nature.

It was at this point that we stopped trying to get pregnant. Adoption was our chosen option. We both figured that if we could love this four-legged daughter as much as we did, then loving a child not of our bodies would be easy.

The adoption wait started.

Harmony watched as we bought baby things. As each new bag or box was brought into the house, she inspected each one and sniffed her approval. Her favorite was the vibrating cradle. It stood six inches off the ground and played music and ocean sounds and vibrated. She'd curl up in it each night as we watched TV or played board games.

We wanted to give Harmony an idea of how it would be with a baby in the house, so we brought home a baby doll that cried and had a heartbeat. We dressed it in a set of my friend's daughter's clothes so that it would smell like a real baby, and we introduced Harmony to it. She sniffed the doll and licked its face, and when we laid it in the cradle, she jumped in and lay quietly at its feet. She was fine with that new addition.

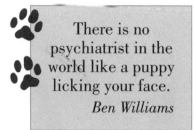

There is no psychiatrist in the world like a puppy licking your face.

Ben Williams

The adoption wait continued. For the next two years, we took a ride on a mental, physical, and emotional roller coaster. Harmony was an anchor for us. In our darkest moments she would jump on our laps, give us a kiss, and lean her body in as close to ours as she could get. It was impossible to stay gloomy when this little point of light stepped into the room.

One day the call came. Our lawyer had a baby boy for us. George and I fought battling emotions. We weren't spring chickens anymore. We were almost six years older than when this journey started. Could we raise a little boy? Would we have the strength and stamina? We'd be retirement age by the time he reached marrying age. All the doubts filtered through our minds.

As the clash of questions ruled us through the night, Harmony just moved quietly from one lap to another. She'd lean back and stare into our faces intently as if to say, "It's never too late, guys. Go for it!"

By morning we told our lawyer yes.

Soon the kitten-like cries of a little baby filled our home, and Harmony had a brother. She would follow us around from room to room and stare at the baby's face.

As our new child grew, Harmony's condition became harder and harder to control. Her glucose levels were all over the board. They'd be high one day and very low the next. We were unsure about correct dosages. She was sleeping more and playing less.

Then one day I watched her walk into a wall. My heart broke when her doctor confirmed my suspicion that Harmony was blind. She'd gone blind almost overnight. I was told it was common in her condition. Soon after, I started diapering two babies. Harmony was unable to control her urine. I took newborn diapers and cut a little hole out of the back for her tail. I'd lay both of my "babies" on their backs on the bed and diaper each one.

When our son, Keefer, was a year and a half, Harmony's diabetes went completely out of control. Even in the twenty-four-hour environment of hospitalization, her levels couldn't be controlled. We were not yet ready to put her down. We brought her home.

Over the next few months we watched our son grow in empathy. He would come to me and say,

"Harmony sick. She need kiss." He'd then hold her little head between his tiny hands and plant a kiss right on her lips. I'd also find them curled up in a blanket in front of the TV, Harmony's head lying on Keefer's arm.

"Shhh!" Keefer would say. "She asleep." He made sure the blanket was tucked closely around Harmony's body.

Finally one evening, the day before my birthday, I carried Harmony into Keefer's room so that he could kiss her good night.

"She sad, Mommy," he said after his kiss.

"Yes. She sad."

After shutting the door to my son's room, I took Harmony into my bedroom and sat down on the edge of the bed. George was already in bed, and he watched me. As I looked into Harmony's cloudy gray eyes, her heart spoke to me. It was time. She was ready to go.

The next day we wrapped her in her pink blanket and took her to the hospital for the final time. Afterward Keefer looked at us and said, "Harmony dead."

Yes, Harmony was dead, but her spirit was living in all of us. She was the "first child," Keefer's first buddy, and our friend. Without her, our transition from single to married to parents would have been much tougher. What amazes me most is that she held on through all the critical medical moments until she was sure that we had a baby to take her place. She was much stronger than most humans I know.

A tuft of Harmony's hair hangs encased in a clear bulb on our Christmas tree each year. She will never be forgotten.

A Dog and His Boy

Mark Ozeroff

Mulligan. My youngest brother certainly has an odd name. Out of the four of us boys, he's the apple of our parents' eye. I never blamed them a bit for feeling this way; Mulligan has a beguiling personality, he's smart as a whip, and he's by far the best looking of us. He's my hirsute, quadruped sibling—Mulligan is a dog.

When I was a kid, we always had animals around: cats, dogs, turtles, and rats were to be found in various combinations. But the premier pet was a West Highland white terrier named Angus; when he succumbed to old age, my mother could not bring herself to get another dog. Twenty years and retirement intervened before my folks decided to take the plunge again. They roamed Florida before running across a weanling Westie pup, and that was it—Mulligan wriggled his way into their hearts, then their household.

Westies are among the most mischievous crea-
tures in existence, and Mulligan is no exception. It's
a full-time battle keeping up with his depredations.
Within half an hour of his rising in the morning, dog
toys and rawhide bones turn the living room into a
canine playground. After Mom vacuums the carpet,
the multitude of tiny hoofprints that spontaneously
appear make it seem that an entire herd of dogs has
galloped through. To get any peace at night, my folks
had to train the dog to sleep in a kennel.

Mulligan has rules; one of them is that anyone
who comes near his stuffed hedgehog has to throw
it, the harder the better. He'll chase it down, straining
desperately to catch it before movement stops. He'll
shake it as hard as possible until it clouts him on both
sides of his head; that he doesn't have cauliflower
ears seems a miracle. Then the hedgehog fight is on
as, growling furiously, Mulligan wages a tug-of-war
for all he's worth. He never stops until he's so tired
he simply falls over and goes to sleep.

Mulligan's level of intelligence is almost scary. He
can intuit human thought with a single glance of his
soulful dark eyes. When spoken to, he'll cock his head
knowingly. His canine vocabulary is impressive too,
ranging from sharp, one-hundred-decibel barks to
gently whining laments.

His method of greeting my father was singular.
When Pop came through the garage door, Mulligan
would roll out an extended *whoo-oo-oo* while joyously
performing the dog dance. My father always stooped

to affectionately ruffle a patch of fur, accepting the inevitable tail-whipping in return.

Unlike Mom, Pop never had pets as a child. He made up for lost time, though, when Mulligan arrived on scene; my father and Mulligan instantly bonded. It was almost as though Pop entered a second childhood. He and his diminutive companion comprised a six-legged entity, roaming the

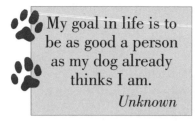

> My goal in life is to be as good a person as my dog already thinks I am.
>
> *Unknown*

neighborhood and courting innocent trouble.

For instance, Pop would sometimes return from a walk with Mulligan liberally covered in burrs and stickers. When accosted by Mom, they'd double-team her—my dad would stammer an explanation while the dog assumed an apologetic expression sure to soften the hardest heart. Such episodes never prevented the recurrence of further boyish mischief, often on the same day.

If these two weren't to be found walking the neighborhood, they were cruising more widely in a golf cart, one chasing distant and tantalizing odors while the other vicariously enjoyed the experience. Everyone for a mile in all directions knew the dog and his seventy-year-old boy. When Pop and Mulligan tired from the day's play, they'd nap next to one another, fond hand trailing from couch to dog.

My mother idly commented one day that Pop looked jaundiced. A physician's examination brought dreadful news—my dad had pancreatic cancer. He opted to submit to a Whipple procedure, a most complicated operation. As he recovered in the ICU, Pop initially seemed to have tolerated the surgery well.

Pop's absence had a palpable effect on the dog; Mulligan pined for his man, even while comforting his woman. The degree of moral support that he provided my mom was astonishing; even we boys were incapable of helping her more. Though Mulligan may not always exhibit the best behavior, his intentions are above reproach.

As rapidly as possible, Pop was sprung from the hospital to recuperate at home. Mulligan's ecstasy upon my dad's return was boundless; never had the dog rendered his dance with such enthusiasm. He took up station, watching over Pop from his bedside post. I'm not sure who gained more comfort from the proximity, man or beast.

If he was initially puzzled by the inactivity of his human, Mulligan soon did that at which animals excel—he adapted to change. Pop had to use a walker to get around, and the dog moved cautiously around him. Walks that previously had ranged far and wide now were restricted to the house. On the rare occasions Pop was able to take Mulligan into the yard, Mulligan was uncharacteristically circumspect. Where once he'd towed Pop around by the leash like a Mack truck with a trailer, the dog now restrained himself.

But the surgery proved unequal to the task; Pop's cancer metastasized, necessitating a return to the

Bec's Biscuits

You can make your own dog biscuits. Try this genuine dog-tested recipe.

1 10.5 oz. can of gravy (any flavor)
1 egg
2 c. wheat flour
1 c. wheat germ
1 T. garlic powder (optional)

Preheat oven to 300 degrees. Mix all ingredients together. Pat into 11-by-17-inch jellyroll pan (a cookie sheet with sides) coated with cooking spray. Score into one-inch squares with a paring knife. Bake for 30 to 45 minutes or until the edges are golden brown and the center is firm. Cool on a cooling rack, then break into pieces.

For Fido's Sweet Tooth
Another excellent treat for dogs? Baby carrots. Why? They're crunchy, they're sweet, they're veterinarian-approved, and best of all, they're excellent roughage for your dog.

hospital. On the night my once-robust father slipped into a coma, Mulligan was unsettled, reluctant to use his kennel. Instinctively he sensed that matters were coming to a head. The following day, Pop passed away; when Mom returned home, Mulligan refused to leave her side. He's never since slept in his kennel.

The dog has taken it upon himself to watch over her day and night. It's almost as though he's assumed one of the jobs my dad performed so well for forty-seven years: that of protector. Woe betide the man who would threaten Mom, for he would find powerful jaws locked stubbornly on him.

I've always been aware of the effect our pets have on us, but what's only just become clear is the elemental pull we exert on them. We recently observed another *yahrzeit*, the anniversary of death as reckoned by the Jewish calendar. Four years after Pop died, it's obvious that memories of my father run strong through the dog's mind.

Mulligan still waits by the door for his favorite boy to come home.

Charlie
Brendalyn Crudup Martin

Everything was going wrong. My car broke down, so I had to arrange transportation to work. It was the middle of summer, and the heat was not helping my temper. Still, I should have paid more attention to the signs.

Pixie, my Chihuahua mix, was acting strange. She was normally crazy about my son James, allowing him to dress her up in everything from a birthday hat to a sweater and scarf. Lately she avoided him, and today she snapped at him. After I reassured my son that Pixie still loved him but must be agitated by the heat—I knew I was—I turned my attention back to the lump of metal I was silently cursing.

That night I noticed Pixie was rather listless. She stayed close to me, content just to have me near and not wanting anyone else to bother her. Since the vet had given her a clean bill of health a little over a month ago, I was not too concerned. She didn't eat strange food or take food from strangers, and whenever we sprayed the yard, we made sure she did not come in contact with any of it. Still, she was getting older, and everybody slows down with time. Besides, this heat was about to drive me crazy.

The next day my car was finally fixed, and at least my spirits were up. When James came in asking for food and a dish I didn't want, I knew something was up. Following him into the front yard, I saw a beautiful caramel and white collie. He was sitting between my yard and my neighbor's, his tongue hanging down as he made short pants.

"Mom, this is Charlie. He's hungry and doesn't have a place to stay. Can he stay with us?"

I stared at the collie, knowing what my husband would say, and gently shook my head. "Honey, you know your dad and I agreed to have only one dog."

"But we used to have two dogs."

"I'm sorry. We have Pixie, and that's our limit for now. But you can give Charlie some food and water. Then he needs to go home."

"He doesn't have a home. He just lives in the neighborhood."

I took a closer look at Charlie, noting the clean coat and white teeth and nails. He did not look like a dog living on the streets.

"He's too clean to be homeless, James. Take him back to his street. He'll find his way home." I felt a twinge of guilt. Everyone knew I had a soft spot for

What's Good and Right

The puppies were born two weeks before September 11, 2001. I visited the barn almost daily to talk to Ruby, our chocolate lab, and to cuddle her brood of satiny black puppies. But after September 11, the puppies became more than just seven little squirming bundles sent to entertain us. They represented life and peace and safety: all the things torn from our country in a senseless act of violence.

My family and I spent hours with those puppies, letting their exuberance and love of life heal our hearts and souls. For a moment in time, life became crystal clear. It's not about the hustle and bustle of the outside world but about family, about laughter, about being delighted by the simple gifts life has to offer.

It's about puppies.

Our puppies became a gentle reminder of what's good and right in this world, and I'm glad my family experienced that reminder at a time when we needed it most.

~ Pam Hillman

animals, especially dogs. Growing up in Arkansas, we always had a dog. My love for them seemed to have passed down to my son.

James led Charlie away and was gone for half an hour. When he came back, Charlie was trailing behind.

I stood in the doorway with my arms crossed, waiting to launch into a lecture on obedience.

"I took him to the street I first saw him on, but he won't stay. He just kept following me. I asked around but no one recognized him."

I turned my scolding on Charlie, who just flashed me an "I just want to be friends" smile. "Your dad won't be happy if Charlie's still here when he gets home," I said to James. I walked into the kitchen to finish dinner, hoping Charlie would take the hint and leave.

When Ron got home and came indoors, I felt my hopes dashed. "Whose dog is that between the houses?" he asked.

"That's Charlie. He seems to be the neighborhood mascot."

"Well, he'd better find another place to hang around. I'm getting ready to water the yard, so he'd better get moving."

I glanced out the door as Ron turned on the water hose and noticed Charlie had slipped behind the hedges of the yard next door. With the temperature so high, the ground was dry in half an hour. When I looked out again, Charlie had taken his position between the houses, almost as if standing guard. He watched James and the other kids play and occasionally joined them, chasing the ball and the kids, then running off with the ball so they had to chase him.

This schedule kept up for several days. Sometime during the day, Charlie would wander off for a while, then come back and take his station when the kids were out and playing. Each evening he would lie down between the houses, barking at anyone who got too close to our house, which was driving Ron crazy. Several times he shouted out the window for Charlie to be quiet. Charlie was smart enough to know when to get out of the way and when it was safe to come back.

> Don't accept your dog's admiration as conclusive evidence that you are wonderful.
>
> *Ann Landers*

During this time, Pixie was still listless. She only wanted to be with me. She would eat if I fed her but otherwise avoided everyone else. I made an appointment with the vet for a couple of days later and went about my usual routine, with the exception of sneaking food to Charlie. Somehow I had allowed myself to be drafted into the conspiracy to add another dog to our household.

By the time we went to the vet, Pixie would hardly move. Her breathing was labored, her eyes glazed. As I held her trembling body in my arms, I looked into tortured eyes and realized how deep my feelings ran for her and hers for me. Sitting in the veterinarian's office, I gently rocked her back and forth. The vet took her into the infirmary, hooked her up to IVs, and began to run tests, but it was too late. She passed away.

With my arms wrapped around my son, I wept tears of pain mixed with anger. Anger at myself and even at the vet for not knowing something was wrong. When he finished his examination, he told us, "She died from a fast-growing cancer. There were no signs when she came in last month. It grew so fast, there was nothing anyone could have done."

Somehow that didn't help. Our trip home was silent. We were both stunned by Pixie's sudden death.

The first thing we saw when we pulled into the driveway was Charlie. He stood quietly for a moment, as if sensing our pain, then ran up to James and nudged his hand. James put his arms around him and looked up at me.

"I'll talk to your dad," I replied.

I had several talks with Ron, trying to convince him to allow Charlie to stay, but in the end, it wasn't anything James or I said, it was Charlie himself who won Ron over.

When Ron walked outside to get a good look at Charlie, I followed, a silent prayer on my lips. They stood and looked at each other for several seconds. Finally Ron said, "He's a smart dog. See how he looks me in the eye. Most dogs don't do that. You can keep him, but he has to go in the backyard. No more sleeping between the houses."

Charlie took to his new home like he'd been there always. During the day he stayed in the yard or the laundry room, which had a doggie door to the backyard. When James came home from school, the first thing he would do was let Charlie out, and they would race through the neighborhood.

Gradually, over time, the loss of Pixie was healed through Charlie's love, and James was finally able to let go of the hurt. As the months passed, the one-year anniversary of Charlie joining us drew near. I laughingly told James I would have to bake Charlie a cake. When we came home one evening, James rushed to the laundry room to let Charlie out, but he was not there. Nor was he anywhere in the yard.

We found no signs to show how he got out, but he was gone. After combing the neighborhood for hours, we gave up and hoped he would show up later. The next day we expected to find him sitting between the houses, but we were disappointed. We searched the neighboring streets and asked the kids around the area if they'd seen Charlie, but nobody had.

By the end of the week, we stopped looking. Charlie had disappeared as suddenly as he had appeared one year ago. I could tell James was upset. He did not understand why Charlie left the way he did.

"Mom, he didn't even say good-bye. Why would he leave? I thought he was happy here."

"Maybe someone else needed him more than you," I replied.

"What do you mean?"

I sat down next to him and said, "Remember how Charlie showed up a few days before Pixie died?"

He nodded his head.

"It almost seemed like he knew you would need him," I continued. "Well, over the past year, you've let go of your grief over Pixie and become involved more with your friends. Maybe Charlie stayed until he knew you were okay."

James thought this over a moment, then asked, "Was Charlie an angel dog?"

"Maybe he was," I replied, hoping that would help him get over Charlie's leaving.

"I still wish he had said good-bye," James said before going out to play with his friends.

"So do I," I whispered.

A few days passed, and I was returning home from the store when I spotted Charlie walking toward our house. I pulled the car over and opened the rear passenger door. "Charlie, get in," I called. He leaped into the car and sprawled on the seat, that familiar doggie smile on his face.

"Where have you been?" I asked, as if expecting him to answer. He only smiled back at me. When we reached the house, I opened the door, and Charlie jumped out, racing across the street to greet James. After a little scolding and lots of pats and hugs, they raced together through the neighborhood as if Charlie had never left.

When they returned later that evening, James stayed in the backyard a while playing with Charlie, making up for lost time.

The next morning, Charlie was gone. When James went to feed him before going to school, the backyard was empty. We stood in amazement, not sure what to make of it, when James suddenly said, "Charlie didn't come back to stay; he came to say good-bye. He really must be an angel dog."

We never saw Charlie again. This time he had really vanished. Despite offers of a reward, no one came forward to say they had seen him, and none of the shelters had a dog fitting his description. I guess we'll never know for sure, but I suspect that somewhere another young boy or girl who had lost someone special suddenly found themselves looking into the smiling eyes of an angel named Charlie.

King Brutus

Carmen Leal

He was as an engaging puppy. His big, brown puppy eyes begged us to keep him. His champagne-colored fur, the color of fur some women pay fortunes for, was soft and silky.

"Can we keep him, Mom? We'll never be bad again. We'll take care of him ourselves. You won't even know he's here!"

My two little sons spouted every promise a little boy can dream of in the space of three minutes. For years their father and I had succeeded as a united front against becoming pet owners. Now Dad no longer lived at home. Divorce rent the very fabric of my children's lives, a jagged tear that threatened to last forever. Time had passed, and now I was ready to begin anew. Whereas the children were still upset, I had healed sufficiently and had even gone through the excitement of falling in love again. David was the perfect man who would make the perfect husband. He had only one flaw—he loved dogs.

Each reason my boys gave for wanting a dog, David echoed and added one of his own. These sons of mine had not been too sure about Dave. They'd been acting as a united hedge around Mom to protect her from this interloper. But now their defense had a crack, and the three males banded together to persuade me to keep the dog. Under the weight of their pleas, I finally crumbled. The boys, spurred on by the thrill of ownership, rocketed to get their puppy.

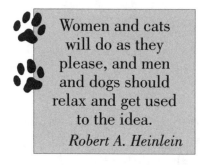

Women and cats will do as they please, and men and dogs should relax and get used to the idea.

Robert A. Heinlein

Brutus had a peaceful first night. We didn't even hear a peep from him. Half standard poodle and half golden retriever, he was 100 percent adorable.

The trouble began with Brutus eating my mother's white shoes, purchased especially for my wedding. A rush to the hardware store for white paint along with a "Bad dog, bad dog!" took care of both problems.

But the fun really started after the wedding. It seemed no matter what we tried, we simply could not train him. To conquer the problem, the boys and David eagerly trotted Brutus off to obedience training each Wednesday.

As bright as this bundle of joy was, the minute he walked into our home, it became his territory. Brutus quickly discovered that during the day the house was his kingdom, and he was King Brutus. As we worked and studied, Brutus frolicked through his castle, ate shoes and other delectable belongings, devoured any food left in sight, and generally wreaked havoc on his surroundings.

No matter what we tried, this was a dog out of our control. The glass-topped coffee table near the window became his throne, where he sunned himself each day. His throne crashed one day—because of his ever-increasing weight—leaving shards of glass strewn around the floor. Brutus sat cowering, waiting for the phrase he'd so often hear: "Bad dog! Bad dog!"

Another day the wind slammed the door shut and trapped him in our bedroom. He clawed his way out of the hollow-core door, leaving a two-foot-high, jagged hole in his wake.

Brutus, relentless in his quest for food, discovered an ability to open the refrigerator door. Oh, the glories of food that were his! As if he were doing something wonderful for me, Brutus carted his prizes to *my* side of the bed. He then proceeded to deposit chunks of food, doggie slobber, and other less-than-delightful presents on my bedspread.

Each time I determined to call the pound, the children cried. They would do anything to keep their dog—pay for the damage, train him—please, Mom, please! They even tried using guilt to make their point: first it was Dad, now it's Brutus.

As my guilt increased, so did the pressure to keep the dog. Meanwhile, the damage to my home continued, and I despaired of ever reclaiming domestic peace and tranquility. When the broken door through which he escaped to roam the neighborhood was fixed, Brutus the Wonder Dog discovered the window as an alternative route, despite the glass and screen. Off he went on another exploration.

Finally, there came "the day." Lines had been drawn, and Brutus had crossed them all. The damage, the dirt, the incessant barking all contributed to one thing: this dog must go. The tears coursed down my sons' faces as they wailed in protest. I was the worst mother in the world. And all the time, as the battle raged, my husband silently sat with an accusing stare. Finally, exhausted, I promised I'd sleep on it and have a decision by morning.

The house grew quiet, and I turned to God for help with my dilemma. As if he were not fully aware of the situation, I pleaded my case, stressing just how bad the situation had become with this eighty-pound terror. I justified my actions, convinced he would agree. But the peace I expected to have once I'd made a decision simply would not come. I tossed and turned until finally I went into the living room to sit on the remains of the sofa Brutus had ravaged.

As I sat close to tears, I peered under the kitchen table—and there was Brutus. His soft snores whistled through the silent house. I weighed my options as the indecision mounted. I cried out my anguish. I knew my sons would survive the loss of Brutus, but would I survive their anger and hurt?

I realized that my experience with Brutus was a mirror image of how God must feel about me so often. The sofa being shredded was no different than the untruths I continued to tell. Crashing through the window and eating the door were like me losing my temper unjustly with my family. No, I hadn't murdered anyone or been unfaithful to my husband, but I was not the woman I should be.

My sons cleaned up after Brutus each time he made a mess. They offered up their allowance to pay for the damages, endured rainy nights to walk him, and listened to endless hours of complaints from neighbors after each barking rampage. Brutus could do no wrong grave enough for them to give him to the pound. They were even willing to plead his case to their mean-spirited, heartless mother. They had an unconditional love at which I marveled.

The love my boys showed for their dog was not dissimilar to the love God has for me. I try to do better and yet I fail. The pain I have caused God over the years is so much greater than the pain Brutus caused me. The lessons Brutus needed to learn seemed so easy, as are the lessons I should learn from God. Brutus should have known he would be fed and protected. And I should trust God. Yet my nemesis and I were alike in our lack of trust.

As these truths set in, I was filled with love and thankfulness. I saw Brutus in a new light. I realized that if God had the patience and understanding for me, I could show those qualities to Brutus.

Brutus lived at our house until we moved to a new state thousands of miles away. As he matured, he learned more and made fewer mistakes. I hope I am doing the same. We still had ups and downs with Brutus, and I was never as forgiving with Brutus as God is with me. But every so often, as I find myself headed in the wrong direction, I remember Brutus and think twice about my destination.

Thanks, Brutus.

Acknowledgments

Many thanks to the talented and patient writers in this book who gave me the privilege of using their stories.

Many more thanks to the wonderful people at Revell, a division of Baker Publishing Group, who worked hard to make this book a reality.

Notes

1. Jack London, *The Call of the Wild* (New York: Grosset & Dunlap, 1903), 169–70.

2. Ibid., 173.

3. Amy Sacks, "Pet Owners Gladly Pay for Veterinary Insurance," *Jackson Citizen Patriot*, March 3, 2007.

4. Robert Hudson and Shelley Townsend, *The Animal Muse* (Grand Rapids: Perciphery Press, 1988), 5. Used by permission.

5. Ibid., 9.

6. Ibid., 3.

Contributors

Chad Allen is an acquisitions editor for Baker Books and a freelance writer. His articles have appeared in *PRISM ePistle, Radix, Regeneration Quarterly,* and *Relevant.* He lives with his wife Alyssa and their son Lucas in Grand Rapids, Michigan.

Twila Bennett is the senior marketing director for a book publisher. Her stories have been published in *MomSense* magazine and in several books. She and her husband Dan enjoy their bright red speedboat every summer on Michigan lakes with their son, Zach. Every night she cuddles with her spoiled dog Tyson—a boxer who never listens to a word she says but whom she completely adores.

Virginia Bowen is a former dog trainer who has taken her lifelong love of animals to the level of all-consuming passion, recently moving from suburban Los Angeles to a 670-acre horse and cattle ranch in "the Texas boonies." There, in addition to having "the most pampered show cattle on earth," Virginia enjoys enriching the lives of her four donkeys, five horses, and Catahoula Leopard cattle dog. She is working on her B.S. in biology and an eventual Ph.D. focused on animal cognition and behavior in order to ultimately help better the welfare of all domesticated animals.

Melody Carlson is a full-time writer and the much-loved author of over two hundred books for teens, adults, and children, including the recent holiday book *An Irish Christmas*. She and her husband live in Oregon and travel together as often as they can wherever they may.

Candace Carteen is a prolific short story writer whose work can be found in *Chicken Soup for the Soul, God Allows U-Turns, Cup of Comfort*, and many other anthologies. She also speaks and teaches the art of storytelling. She currently lives in Ocean Park, Washington, with her husband, her son, two dogs, two cats, two fish, and a family of raccoons.

Lonnie Hull DuPont is a poet and book editor living in rural Michigan. Her poetry can be read in dozens of periodicals and literary journals, and her work has been nominated for a Pushcart Prize. She is author of *The Haiku Box*.

Julianne Dwelle is the pseudonym for a writer of nonfiction who adores animals of all kinds.

Nancy Jo Eckerson, a professional writer and ethical wills facilitator, lives in a tiny farm town in western New York. Nancy is a great lover of nature—both Mother Nature and human nature—and she is devoted to making a positive difference here on Earth. She will be honored if her writing brings you a smile.

Shane Galloway is a writer and actor who now rents in the Midtown area of Sacramento, California, where he no longer has to worry about broken sprinkler heads, dry rot, squirrels in the attic, and other troubles that once came with owning a home. He is currently writing a memoir about his experiences growing up in the church.

Callie Smith Grant is the author of several books for young readers and adults as well as many animal-themed stories and poems that can be seen in Guideposts anthologies and in magazines such as *Small Farm Journal*.

Joan Lloyd Guest is a licensed clinical social worker specializing in geriatric issues and marriage work. She spent over twenty years in Christian publishing before changing careers. Along with work at the Elderday Center adult daycare, Joan offers specialized marital therapy through her church. Her great gift of a dog died in the arms of his loving family just a few years after he came to them.

Kristi Hemingway is a teacher, performer, freelance writer, and staff writer for *Kids' Pages*. She writes curriculum for theater, speech, and creative drama courses, and she has published with several children's and family magazines, including *Breakaway*, *On the Line*, *Brio & Beyond*, and *Parentingteacher*. She lives in Denver with her wonderful husband; two lovely children, Levi and Eden; and a Yorkshire terrier named Miette who is pretty much queen of the castle.

Pam Hillman is a multipublished author in short fiction and nonfiction and continues to stretch her wings as a writer of inspirational fiction set in the American West. The code of the West has always resonated with the internal fabric on which Pam was raised: that of hard work, honesty, and being a good neighbor. Born in the heart of Mississippi and a hundred years too late, Pam still boasts of wrangling calves, milking cows, and cuddling puppies.

Bernadine Johnson is grateful that God has given her the opportunity to be a wife, mother, grandmother, teacher, musician, friend, and dog owner. Since graduating from Indiana Wesleyan University, she has been working in the field of music, teaching piano along with writing music and articles for publication. She lives in Fremont, Michigan, with her husband Bob and collie Maggie.

Deb Kalmbach is an author and speaker and the coauthor of *Because I Said Forever: Embracing Hope in a Not-So-Perfect Marriage*. She and her husband Randy live in Washington's beautiful Methow Valley with their lively Jack Russell terriers, Kramer and Kosmo. Their grown sons Chris and Jeremy live in the Seattle area.

Kathryn Lay is a full-time writer for children and adults. She lives in Arlington, Texas, where she and her family—including their dog, Penny—enjoy spending time together.

Carmen Leal is the author of nine books, including *The Twenty-Third Psalm for Caregivers* and *The Twenty-Third Psalm for Those Who Grieve*. A popular presenter at conventions, conferences, and church groups throughout the United States, she lives with her family in Kailua, Hawaii.

Bonnie Leon is the author of fifteen novels, including the popular Queensland Chronicles, the Sydney Cove series, and the bestselling *Journey of Eleven Moons*. She also stays busy speaking and teaching at writing seminars and conventions. Bonnie and her husband Greg live in Oregon. They have three grown children and four grandchildren.

Brendalyn Crudup Martin was appointed Poet Laureate of the Arizona Supreme Court in 1996 by Justice Stanley Feldon. She is a writer of poetry, devotionals, and children's stories. She is a wife, mother, and grandmother who uses her children as inspiration for some of her stories. An ordained minister in the Christian Methodist Church, she serves as associate assistant at Phillips Memorial CME Church in Phoenix, Arizona.

Marilyn Martyn McAuley is the author of numerous works, including personal experience stories in various anthologies and a series for toddlers, and she is coauthor of an inspirational book. She and her husband, Dan, had two more German shepherds after Schoen and currently enjoy the delightful antics of their two-year-old miniature schnauzer, Bailey.

Diane Nichols is a single mother to two beautiful girls and a full-time newspaper reporter in Winter Haven, Florida. She is also the author of *Prison of My Own*, a true story of redemption and forgiveness after her husband of thirteen years murdered his mistress. *The Christian Marketplace* called the book "the most amazing story to come along in over thirty years."

Mark Ozeroff holds the written word in high enough esteem to have been a writer for five years. Until this point, he'd managed to sell 297 of the 1,230,000 words he's written. Having completed a World War II novel and a raft of stories and essays, he is currently working on a manuscript involving the Vietnam War. Mark finds what consolation he can in counting himself among the most erudite of bums.

Robert Lloyd Russell's career included management positions in engineering, sales, marketing, and manufacturing. He then managed his own management advisory firm for many years before retiring. He and his wife live in the Pacific Northwest and are active in their church and other local activities.

Hilary Walker is English and moved to the States six years ago. Together with her horses, cats, husband, son, and four dogs, she currently lives, writes, and rides in Calvert County, Maryland. Her dog Blue made it clear to Hilary how indispensable his breed is to her happiness. Her current Great Dane is Chloe, a fawn female who bounces around the house and grounds, exuding energy and affection and continuing where Blue left off.

Laura Jensen Walker is an award-winning author who writes humorous fiction and nonfiction. Her books include novels *Miss Invisible* and *Reconstructing Natalie* and nonfiction *Thanks for the Mammogram!* and *Mentalpause*. She and her husband Michael are the "people" of Gracie, their spoiled but adorable American Eskimo canine daughter.

Michael K. Walker is a former vocational actor who dabbles in many art forms. He is married to author Laura Jensen Walker, with whom he cowrote a Christmas-for-grown-ups book, *God Rest Ye Grumpy Scroogeymen*. Michael and Laura share their home with their American Eskimo dog-child, Gracie.

Anne C. Watkins is the author of *The Conure Handbook* as well as scores of nonfiction articles and essays for publications such as *Chicken Soup for the Soul, Cup of Comfort, Guideposts, Angels on Earth, Pet Age, Reminisce,* and numerous others. She and her husband Allen live in Alabama.

Heartwarming
stories of
the cats we love

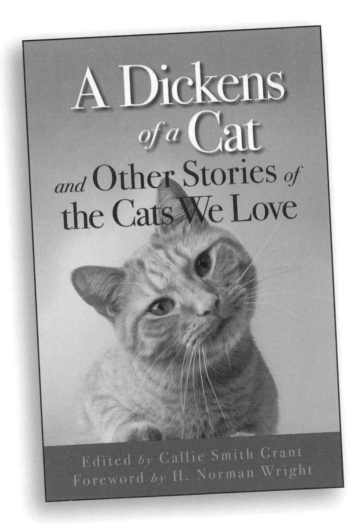

A Dickens
of a Cat

and Other Stories *of*
the Cats We Love

Edited *by* Callie Smith Grant
Foreword *by* H. Norman Wright

 Revell

a division of Baker Publishing Group